Protecting Consumer Privacy in an Era of Rapid Change

RECOMMENDATIONS FOR
BUSINESSES AND POLICYMAKERS

FTC REPORT
MARCH 2012

CONTENTS

EXECUTIVE SUMMARY

In today's world of smart phones, smart grids, and smart cars, companies are collecting, storing, and sharing more information about consumers than ever before. Although companies use this information to innovate and deliver better products and services to consumers, they should not do so at the expense of consumer privacy.

With this Report, the Commission calls on companies to act now to implement best practices to protect consumers' private information. These best practices include making privacy the "default setting" for commercial data practices and giving consumers greater control over the collection and use of their personal data through simplified choices and increased transparency. Implementing these best practices will enhance trust and stimulate commerce.

This Report follows a preliminary staff report that the Federal Trade Commission ("FTC" or "Commission") issued in December 2010. The preliminary report proposed a framework for protecting consumer privacy in the 21st Century. Like this Report, the framework urged companies to adopt the following practices, consistent with the Fair Information Practice Principles first articulated almost 40 years ago:

- ◆ **Privacy by Design:** Build in privacy at every stage of product development;
- ◆ **Simplified Choice for Businesses and Consumers:** Give consumers the ability to make decisions about their data at a relevant time and context, including through a Do Not Track mechanism, while reducing the burden on businesses of providing unnecessary choices; and
- ◆ **Greater Transparency:** Make information collection and use practices transparent.

The Commission received more than 450 public comments in response to the preliminary report from various stakeholders, including businesses, privacy advocates, technologists and individual consumers. A wide range of stakeholders, including industry, supported the principles underlying the framework, and many companies said they were already following them. At the same time, many commenters criticized the slow pace of self-regulation, and argued that it is time for Congress to enact baseline privacy legislation. In this Report, the Commission addresses the comments and sets forth a revised, final privacy framework that adheres to, but also clarifies and fine-tunes, the basic principles laid out in the preliminary report.

Since the Commission issued the preliminary staff report, Congress has introduced both general privacy bills and more focused bills, including ones addressing Do Not Track and the privacy of teens. Industry has made some progress in certain areas, most notably, in responding to the preliminary report's call for Do Not Track. In other areas, however, industry progress has been far slower. Thus, overall, consumers do not yet enjoy the privacy protections proposed in the preliminary staff report.

The Administration and certain Members of Congress have called for enactment of baseline privacy legislation. The Commission now also calls on Congress to consider enacting baseline privacy legislation and reiterates its call for data security legislation. The Commission is prepared to work with Congress and other stakeholders to craft such legislation. At the same time, the Commission urges industry to accelerate the pace of self-regulation.

The remainder of this Executive Summary describes key developments since the issuance of the preliminary report, discusses the most significant revisions to the proposed framework, and lays out several next steps.

DEVELOPMENTS SINCE ISSUANCE OF THE PRELIMINARY REPORT

In the last 40 years, the Commission has taken numerous actions to shape the consumer privacy landscape. For example, the Commission has sued dozens of companies that broke their privacy and security promises, scores of telemarketers that called consumers on the Do Not Call registry, and more than a hundred scammers peddling unwanted spam and spyware. Since it issued the initial staff report, the Commission has redoubled its efforts to protect consumer privacy, including through law enforcement, policy advocacy, and consumer and business education. It has also vigorously promoted self-regulatory efforts.

On the law enforcement front, since December 2010, the Commission:

♦ Brought enforcement actions against Google and Facebook. The orders obtained in these cases require the companies to obtain consumers' affirmative express consent before materially changing certain of their data practices and to adopt strong, company-wide privacy programs that outside auditors will assess for 20 years. These orders will protect the more than one billion Google and Facebook users worldwide.

♦ Brought enforcement actions against online advertising networks that failed to honor opt outs. The orders in these cases are designed to ensure that when consumers choose to opt out of tracking by advertisers, their choice is effective.

♦ Brought enforcement actions against mobile applications that violated the Children's Online Privacy Protection Act as well as applications that set default privacy settings in a way that caused consumers to unwittingly share their personal data.

♦ Brought enforcement actions against entities that sold consumer lists to marketers in violation of the Fair Credit Reporting Act.

♦ Brought actions against companies for failure to maintain reasonable data security.

On the policy front, since December 2010, the FTC and staff:

♦ Hosted two privacy-related workshops, one on child identity theft and one on the privacy implications of facial recognition technology.

♦ Testified before Congress ten times on privacy and data security issues.

♦ Consulted with other federal agencies, including the Federal Communications Commission, the Department of Health and Human Services, and the Department of Commerce, on their privacy initiatives. The Commission has supported the Department of Commerce's initiative to convene stakeholders to develop privacy-related codes of conduct for different industry sectors.

♦ Released a survey of data collection disclosures by mobile applications directed to children.

♦ Proposed amendments to the Children's Online Privacy Protection Act Rule.

On the education front, since December 2010, the Commission:

- ♦ Continued outreach efforts through the FTC's consumer online safety portal, OnGuardOnline.gov, which provides information in a variety of formats – articles, games, quizzes, and videos – to help consumers secure their computers and protect their personal information. It attracts approximately 100,000 unique visitors per month.

- ♦ Published new consumer education materials on identity theft, Wi-Fi hot spots, cookies, and mobile devices.

- ♦ Sent warning letters to marketers of mobile apps that do background checks on individuals, educating them about the requirements of the Fair Credit Reporting Act.

To promote self-regulation, since December 2010, the Commission:

- ♦ Continued its call for improved privacy disclosures and choices, particularly in the area of online behavioral tracking. In response to this call, as well as to Congressional interest:

    - ♦ A number of Internet browser vendors developed browser-based tools for consumers to request that websites not track their online activities.

    - ♦ The World Wide Web Consortium, an Internet standard setting organization, is developing a universal web protocol for Do Not Track.

    - ♦ The Digital Advertising Alliance ("DAA"), a coalition of media and marketing organizations, has developed a mechanism, accessed through an icon that consumers can click, to obtain information about and opt out of online behavioral advertising. Additionally, the DAA has committed to preventing the use of consumers' data for secondary purposes like credit and employment and honoring the choices about tracking that consumers make through the settings on their browsers.

- ♦ Participated in the development of enforceable cross-border privacy rules for businesses to harmonize and enhance privacy protection of consumer data that moves between member countries of the forum on Asia Pacific Economic Cooperation.

THE FINAL REPORT

Based upon its analysis of the comments filed on the proposed privacy framework, as well as commercial and technological developments, the Commission is issuing this final Report. The final framework is intended to articulate best practices for companies that collect and use consumer data. These best practices can be useful to companies as they develop and maintain processes and systems to operationalize privacy and data security practices within their businesses. The final privacy framework contained in this Report is also intended to assist Congress as it considers privacy legislation. To the extent the framework goes beyond existing legal requirements, the framework is not intended to serve as a template for law enforcement actions or regulations under laws currently enforced by the FTC. While retaining the proposed framework's fundamental best practices of privacy by design, simplified choice, and greater transparency, the Commission makes revised recommendations in three key areas in response to the comments.

First, the Commission makes changes to the framework's scope. The preliminary report proposed that the privacy framework apply to all commercial entities that collect or use consumer data that can be reasonably linked to a specific consumer, computer, or other device. To address concerns about undue burdens on small businesses, the final framework does not apply to companies that collect only non-sensitive data from fewer than 5,000 consumers a year, provided they do not share the data with third parties. Commenters also expressed concern that, with improvements in technology and the ubiquity of public information, more and more data could be "reasonably linked" to a consumer, computer or device, and that the proposed framework provided less incentive for a business to try to de-identify the data it maintains. To address this issue, the Report clarifies that data is not "reasonably linkable" to the extent that a company: (1) takes reasonable measures to ensure that the data is de-identified; (2) publicly commits not to try to re-identify the data; and (3) contractually prohibits downstream recipients from trying to re-identify the data.

Second, the Commission revises its approach to how companies should provide consumers with privacy choices. To simplify choice for both consumers and businesses, the proposed framework set forth a list of five categories of "commonly accepted" information collection and use practices for which companies need not provide consumers with choice (product fulfillment, internal operations, fraud prevention, legal compliance and public purpose, and first-party marketing). Several business commenters expressed concern that setting these "commonly accepted practices" in stone would stifle innovation. Other commenters expressed the concern that the "commonly accepted practices" delineated in the proposed framework were too broad and would allow a variety of practices to take place without consumer consent.

In response to these concerns, the Commission sets forth a modified approach that focuses on the context of the consumer's interaction with the business. Under this approach, companies do not need to provide choice before collecting and using consumers' data for practices that are consistent with the context of the transaction, consistent with the company's relationship with the consumer, or as required or specifically authorized by law. Although many of the five "commonly accepted practices" identified in the preliminary report would generally meet this standard, there may be exceptions. The Report provides examples of how this new "context of the interaction" standard would apply in various circumstances.

Third, the Commission recommends that Congress consider enacting targeted legislation to provide greater transparency for, and control over, the practices of information brokers. The proposed framework recommended that companies provide consumers with reasonable access to the data the companies maintain about them, proportionate to the sensitivity of the data and the nature of its use. Several commenters discussed in particular the importance of consumers' ability to access information that information brokers have about them. These commenters noted the lack of transparency about the practices of information brokers, who often buy, compile, and sell a wealth of highly personal information about consumers but never interact directly with them. Consumers are often unaware of the existence of these entities, as well as the purposes for which they collect and use data.

The Commission agrees that consumers should have more control over the practices of information brokers and believes that appropriate legislation could help address this goal. Any such legislation could be modeled on a bill that the House passed on a bipartisan basis during the 111th Congress, which included a procedure for consumers to access and dispute personal data held by information brokers.

IMPLEMENTATION OF THE PRIVACY FRAMEWORK

While Congress considers privacy legislation, the Commission urges industry to accelerate the pace of its self-regulatory measures to implement the Commission's final privacy framework. Although some companies have excellent privacy and data security practices, industry as a whole must do better. Over the course of the next year, Commission staff will promote the framework's implementation by focusing its policymaking efforts on five main action items, which are highlighted here and discussed further throughout the report.

- ◆ **Do Not Track:** As discussed above, industry has made significant progress in implementing Do Not Track. The browser vendors have developed tools that consumers can use to signal that they do not want to be tracked; the Digital Advertising Alliance ("DAA") has developed its own icon-based tool and has committed to honor the browser tools; and the World Wide Web Consortium ("W3C") has made substantial progress in creating an international standard for Do Not Track. However, the work is not done. The Commission will work with these groups to complete implementation of an easy-to use, persistent, and effective Do Not Track system.

- ◆ **Mobile:** The Commission calls on companies providing mobile services to work toward improved privacy protections, including the development of short, meaningful disclosures. To this end, FTC staff has initiated a project to update its business guidance about online advertising disclosures. As part of this project, staff will host a workshop on May 30, 2012 and will address, among other issues, mobile privacy disclosures and how these disclosures can be short, effective, and accessible to consumers on small screens. The Commission hopes that the workshop will spur further industry self-regulation in this area.

- ◆ **Data Brokers:** To address the invisibility of, and consumers' lack of control over, data brokers' collection and use of consumer information, the Commission supports targeted legislation – similar to that contained in several of the data security bills introduced in the 112th Congress – that would provide consumers with access to information about them held by a data broker. To further increase transparency, the Commission calls on data brokers that compile data for marketing purposes to explore creating a centralized website where data brokers could (1) identify themselves to consumers and describe how they collect and use consumer data and (2) detail the access rights and other choices they provide with respect to the consumer data they maintain.

- ◆ **Large Platform Providers:** To the extent that large platforms, such as Internet Service Providers, operating systems, browsers, and social media seek, to comprehensively track consumers' online activities, it raises heightened privacy concerns. To further explore privacy and other issues related to this type of comprehensive tracking, FTC staff intends to host a public workshop in the second half of 2012.

♦ **Promoting Enforceable Self-Regulatory Codes:** The Department of Commerce, with the support of key industry stakeholders, is undertaking a project to facilitate the development of sector-specific codes of conduct. FTC staff will participate in that project. To the extent that strong privacy codes are developed, the Commission will view adherence to such codes favorably in connection with its law enforcement work. The Commission will also continue to enforce the FTC Act to take action against companies that engage in unfair or deceptive practices, including the failure to abide by self-regulatory programs they join.

FINAL FTC PRIVACY FRAMEWORK AND IMPLEMENTATION RECOMMENDATIONS

The final privacy framework is intended to articulate best practices for companies that collect and use consumer data. These best practices can be useful to companies as they develop and maintain processes and systems to operationalize privacy and data security practices within their businesses. The final privacy framework contained in this report is also intended to assist Congress as it considers privacy legislation. To the extent the framework goes beyond existing legal requirements, the framework is not intended to serve as a template for law enforcement actions or regulations under laws currently enforced by the FTC.

SCOPE

Final Scope: The framework applies to all commercial entities that collect or use consumer data that can be reasonably linked to a specific consumer, computer, or other device, unless the entity collects only non-sensitive data from fewer than 5,000 consumers per year and does not share the data with third parties.

PRIVACY BY DESIGN

Baseline Principle: Companies should promote consumer privacy throughout their organizations and at every stage of the development of their products and services.

A. The Substantive Principles

Final Principle: Companies should incorporate substantive privacy protections into their practices, such as data security, reasonable collection limits, sound retention and disposal practices, and data accuracy.

B. Procedural Protections to Implement the Substantive Principles

Final Principle: Companies should maintain comprehensive data management procedures throughout the life cycle of their products and services.

SIMPLIFIED CONSUMER CHOICE

Baseline Principle: Companies should simplify consumer choice.

A. Practices That Do Not Require Choice

Final Principle: Companies do not need to provide choice before collecting and using consumer data for practices that are consistent with the context of the transaction or the company's relationship with the consumer, or are required or specifically authorized by law.

To balance the desire for flexibility with the need to limit the types of practices for which choice is not required, the Commission has refined the final framework so that companies engaged in practices consistent with the context of their interaction with consumers need not provide choices for those practices.

B. Companies Should Provide Consumer Choice for Other Practices

Final Principle: For practices requiring choice, companies should offer the choice at a time and in a context in which the consumer is making a decision about his or her data. Companies should obtain affirmative express consent before (1) using consumer data in a materially different manner than claimed when the data was collected; or (2) collecting sensitive data for certain purposes.

The Commission commends industry's efforts to improve consumer control over online behavioral tracking by developing a Do Not Track mechanism, and encourages continued improvements and full implementation of those mechanisms.

TRANSPARENCY

Baseline Principle: Companies should increase the transparency of their data practices.

A. Privacy notices

Final Principle: Privacy notices should be clearer, shorter, and more standardized to enable better comprehension and comparison of privacy practices.

B. Access

Final Principle: Companies should provide reasonable access to the consumer data they maintain; the extent of access should be proportionate to the sensitivity of the data and the nature of its use.

The Commission has amplified its support for this principle by including specific recommendations governing the practices of information brokers.

C. Consumer Education

Final Principle: All stakeholders should expand their efforts to educate consumers about commercial data privacy practices.

LEGISLATIVE RECOMMENDATIONS

The Commission now also calls on Congress to consider enacting baseline privacy legislation and reiterates its call for data security and data broker legislation. The Commission is prepared to work with Congress and other stakeholders to craft such legislation. At the same time, the Commission urges industry to accelerate the pace of self-regulation.

FTC WILL ASSIST WITH IMPLEMENTATION IN FIVE KEY AREAS

As discussed throughout the Commission's final Report, there are a number of specific areas where policy makers have a role in assisting with the implementation of the self-regulatory principles that make up the final privacy framework. Areas where the FTC will be active over the course of the next year include the following:

1. Do Not Track

Industry has made significant progress in implementing Do Not Track. The browser vendors have developed tools that consumers can use to signal that they do not want to be tracked; the DAA has developed its own icon-based tool and has committed to honor the browser tools; and the W3C has made substantial progress in creating an international standard for Do Not Track. However, the work is not done. The Commission will work with these groups to complete implementation of an easy-to use, persistent, and effective Do Not Track system.

2. Mobile

The Commission calls on companies providing mobile services to work toward improved privacy protections, including the development of short, meaningful disclosures. To this end, FTC staff has initiated a project to update its business guidance about online advertising disclosures. As part of this project, staff will host a workshop on May 30, 2012 and will address, among other issues, mobile privacy disclosures and how these disclosures can be short, effective, and accessible to consumers on small screens. The Commission hopes that the workshop will spur further industry self-regulation in this area.

3. Data Brokers

To address the invisibility of, and consumers' lack of control over, data brokers' collection and use of consumer information, the Commission supports targeted legislation – similar to that contained in several of the data security bills introduced in the 112th Congress – that would provide consumers with access to information about them held by a data broker. To further increase transparency, the Commission calls on data brokers that compile data for marketing purposes to explore creating a centralized website where data brokers could (1) identify themselves to consumers and describe how they collect and use consumer data and (2) detail the access rights and other choices they provide with respect to the consumer data they maintain.

4. Large Platform Providers

To the extent that large platforms, such as Internet Service Providers, operating systems, browsers, and social media, seek to comprehensively track consumers' online activities, it raises heightened privacy concerns. To further explore privacy and other issues related to this type of comprehensive tracking, FTC staff intends to host a public workshop in the second half of 2012.

5. Promoting Enforceable Self-Regulatory Codes

The Department of Commerce, with the support of key industry stakeholders, is undertaking a project to facilitate the development of sector-specific codes of conduct. FTC staff will participate in that project. To the extent that strong privacy codes are developed, the Commission will view adherence to such codes favorably in connection with its law enforcement work. The Commission will also continue to enforce the FTC Act to take action against companies that engage in unfair or deceptive practices, including the failure to abide by self-regulatory programs they join.

In all other areas, the Commission calls on individual companies, trade associations, and self-regulatory bodies to adopt the principles contained in the final privacy framework, to the extent they have not already done so. For its part, the FTC will focus its policy efforts on the five areas identified above, vigorously enforce existing laws, work with industry on self-regulation, and continue to target its education efforts on building awareness of existing data collection and use practices and the tools to control them.

I. INTRODUCTION

In December 2010, the Federal Trade Commission ("FTC" or "Commission") issued a preliminary staff report to address the privacy issues associated with new technologies and business models.[1] The report outlined the FTC's 40-year history of promoting consumer privacy through policy and enforcement work, discussed the themes and areas of consensus that emerged from the Commission's "Exploring Privacy" roundtables, and set forth a proposed framework to guide policymakers and other stakeholders regarding best practices for consumer privacy. The proposed framework called on companies to build privacy protections into their business operations (*i.e.*, adopt "privacy by design"[2]), offer simplified choice mechanisms that give consumers more meaningful control, and increase the transparency of their data practices.

The preliminary report included a number of questions for public comment to assist and guide the Commission in developing a final privacy framework. The Commission received more than 450 comments from a wide variety of interested parties, including consumer and privacy advocates, individual companies and trade associations, academics, technologists, and domestic and foreign government agencies. Significantly, more than half of the comments came from individual consumers. The comments have helped the Commission refine the framework to better protect consumer privacy in today's dynamic and rapidly changing marketplace.

In this Final Report, the Commission adopts staff's preliminary framework with certain clarifications and revisions. The final privacy framework is intended to articulate best practices for companies that collect and use consumer data. These best practices can be useful to companies as they develop and maintain processes and systems to operationalize privacy and data security practices within their businesses. The final privacy framework contained in this Report is also intended to assist Congress as it considers privacy legislation. To the extent the framework goes beyond existing legal requirements, the framework is not intended to serve as a template for law enforcement actions or regulations under laws currently enforced by the FTC.

The Report highlights the developments since the FTC issued staff's preliminary report, including the Department of Commerce's parallel privacy initiative, proposed legislation, and actions by industry and other stakeholders. Next, it analyzes and responds to the main issues raised by the public comments. Based on those comments, as well as marketplace developments, the Report sets forth a revised privacy framework and legislative recommendations. Finally, the Report outlines a series of policy initiatives that FTC staff will undertake in the next year to assist industry with implementing the final framework as best practices.

---

1   FTC, *Protecting Consumer Privacy in an Era of Rapid Change, A Proposed Framework for Businesses and Policymakers, Preliminary FTC Staff Report* (Dec. 2010), *available at* http://www.ftc.gov/os/2010/12/101201privacyreport.pdf.

2   Privacy by Design is an approach that Ann Cavoukian, Ph.D., Information and Privacy Commissioner, Ontario, Canada, has advocated. *See* Information and Privacy Commissioner, Ontario, Canada, Privacy by Design, http://privacybydesign.ca/.

II. BACKGROUND

A. FTC ROUNDTABLES AND PRELIMINARY STAFF REPORT

Between December 2009 and March 2010, the FTC convened its "Exploring Privacy" roundtables.[3] The roundtables brought together stakeholders representing diverse interests to evaluate whether the FTC's existing approach to protecting consumer privacy was adequate in light of 21st Century technologies and business models. From these discussions, as well as submitted materials, a number of themes emerged. First, the collection and commercial use of consumer data in today's society is ubiquitous and often invisible to consumers. Second, consumers generally lack full understanding of the nature and extent of this data collection and use and, therefore, are unable to make informed choices about it. Third, despite this lack of understanding, many consumers are concerned about the privacy of their personal information. Fourth, the collection and use of consumer data has led to significant benefits in the form of new products and services. Finally, the traditional distinction between personally identifiable information and "anonymous" data has blurred.

Participants also pointed to shortcomings in existing frameworks that have attempted to address privacy concerns. The "notice-and-choice model," which encouraged companies to develop privacy policies describing their information collection and use practices, led to long, incomprehensible privacy policies that consumers typically do not read, let alone understand.[4] The "harm-based model," which focused on protecting consumers from specific harms – physical security, economic injury, and unwarranted intrusions into their daily lives – had been criticized for failing to recognize a wider range of privacy-related concerns, including reputational harm or the fear of being monitored.[5] Participants noted that both of these privacy frameworks have struggled to keep pace with the rapid growth of technologies and business models that enable companies to collect and use consumers' information in ways that often are invisible to consumers.[6]

Building on the record developed at the roundtables and on its own enforcement and policymaking expertise, FTC staff proposed for public comment a framework for approaching privacy. The proposed framework included three major components. It called on companies to treat privacy as their "default setting" by implementing "privacy by design" throughout their regular business operations. The concept of privacy by design includes limitations on data collection and retention, as well as reasonable security and data accuracy. By considering and addressing privacy at every stage of product and service development,

---

3   The first roundtable took place on December 7, 2009, the second roundtable on January 28, 2010, and the third roundtable on March 17, 2010. *See* FTC, *Exploring Privacy – A Roundtable Series*, http://www.ftc.gov/bcp/workshops/privacyroundtables/index.shtml.

4   *See, e.g., 1st Roundtable, Remarks of Fred Cate, Indiana University Maurer School of Law*, at 280-81; *1st Roundtable, Remarks of Lorrie Cranor, Carnegie Mellon University*, at 129; *see also Written Comment of Fred Cate, 2nd Roundtable, Consumer Protection in the Age of the 'Information Economy,'* cmt. #544506-00057, at 343-79.

5   *See, e.g., 1st Roundtable, Remarks of Marc Rotenberg, Electronic Privacy Information Center*, at 301; *1st Roundtable, Remarks of Leslie Harris, Center for Democracy & Technology*, at 36-38; *1st Roundtable, Remarks of Susan Grant, Consumer Federation of America*, at 38-39.

6   *See, e.g., 3rd Roundtable, Remarks of Kathryn Montgomery, American University School of Communication*, at 200-01; *2nd Roundtable, Remarks of Kevin Bankston, Electronic Frontier Foundation*, at 277.

companies can shift the burden away from consumers who would otherwise have to seek out privacy-protective practices and technologies. The proposed framework also called on companies to simplify consumer choice by presenting important choices – in a streamlined way – to consumers at the time they are making decisions about their data. As part of the call for simplified choice, staff asked industry to develop a mechanism that would allow consumers to more easily control the tracking of their online activities, often referred to as "Do Not Track." Finally, the framework focused on improving consumer understanding of commercial data practices ("transparency") and called on companies – both those that interact directly with consumers and those that lack a consumer interface – to improve the transparency of their practices. As discussed below, the Commission received a large number of thoughtful and informative comments regarding each of the framework's elements. These comments have allowed the Commission to refine the framework and to provide further guidance regarding its implementation.

B. DEPARTMENT OF COMMERCE PRIVACY INITIATIVES

In a related effort to examine privacy, in May 2010, the Department of Commerce ("DOC" or "Commerce") convened a public workshop to discuss how to balance innovation, commerce, and consumer privacy in the online context.[7] Based on the input received from the workshop, as well as related research, on December 16, 2010, the DOC published for comment a strategy paper outlining privacy recommendations and proposed initiatives.[8] Following the public comment period, on February 23, 2012, the Administration issued its final "White Paper" on consumer privacy. The White Paper recommends that Congress enact legislation to implement a Consumer Privacy Bill of Rights based on the Fair Information Practice Principles ("FIPPs").[9] In addition, the White Paper calls for a multistakeholder process to determine how to apply the Consumer Privacy Bill of Rights in different business contexts. Commerce issued a Notice of Inquiry on March 5, 2012, asking for public input on both the process for convening stakeholders on this project, as well as the proposed subject areas to be discussed.[10]

Staff from the FTC and Commerce worked closely to ensure that the agencies' privacy initiatives are complementary. Personnel from each agency actively participated in both the DOC and FTC initiatives, and have also communicated regularly on how best to develop a meaningful, effective, and consistent approach to privacy protection. Going forward, the agencies will continue to work collaboratively to guide implementation of these complementary privacy initiatives.

---

7   *See* Press Release, Department of Commerce, Commerce Secretary Gary Locke Discusses Privacy and Innovation with Leading Internet Stakeholders (May 7, 2010), *available at* http://www.commerce.gov/news/press-releases/2010/05/07/commerce-secretary-gary-locke-discusses-privacy-and-innovation-leadin.

8   *See* Department of Commerce Internet Policy Task Force, *Commercial Data Privacy and Innovation in the Internet Economy: A Dynamic Policy Framework* (Dec. 16, 2010), *available at* http://www.ntia.doc.gov/files/ntia/publications/iptf_privacy_greenpaper_12162010.pdf.

9   White House, *Consumer Data Privacy in a Networked World: A Framework for Protecting Privacy and Promoting Innovation in the Global Digital Economy* (Feb. 2012), *available at* http://www.whitehouse.gov/sites/default/files/privacy-final.pdf. The FIPPs as articulated in the Administration paper are: Transparency, Individual Control, Respect for Context, Security, Access, Accuracy, Focused Collection, and Accountability.

10 *See* National Telecommunications and Information Administration, Request for Public Comment, Multistakeholder Process to Develop Consumer Data Privacy Codes of Conduct, 77 Fed. Reg. 13098 (Mar. 5, 2012).

C. LEGISLATIVE PROPOSALS AND EFFORTS BY STAKEHOLDERS

Since Commission staff released its preliminary report in December 2010, there have been a number of significant legislative proposals, as well as steps by industry and other stakeholders, to promote consumer privacy.

1. DO NOT TRACK

The preliminary staff report called on industry to create and implement a mechanism to allow consumers to control the collection and use of their online browsing data, often referred to as "Do Not Track." Bills introduced in the House and the Senate specifically address the creation of Do Not Track mechanisms, and, if enacted, would mandate that the Commission promulgate regulations to establish standards for a Do Not Track regime.[11]

In addition to the legislative proposals calling for the creation of Do Not Track, staff's preliminary report recommendation triggered significant progress by various industry sectors to develop tools to allow consumers to control online tracking. A number of browser vendors – including Mozilla, Microsoft, and Apple – announced that the latest versions of their browsers permit consumers to instruct websites not to track their activities across websites.[12] Mozilla has also introduced a mobile browser for Android devices that enables Do Not Track.[13] The online advertising industry has also established an important program. The Digital Advertising Alliance ("DAA"), an industry coalition of media and marketing associations, has developed an initiative that includes an icon embedded in behaviorally targeted online ads.[14] When consumers click on the icon, they can see information about how the ad was targeted and delivered to them and they are given the opportunity to opt out of such targeted advertising. The program's recent growth and implementation has been significant. In addition, the DAA has committed to preventing the use of consumers' data for secondary purposes like credit and employment decisions. The DAA has also agreed to honor the choices about tracking that consumers make through settings on their web browsers. This will provide consumers two ways to opt out: through the DAA's icon in advertisements or through their browser settings. These steps demonstrate the online advertising industry's support for privacy and consumer choice.

---

11 *See* Do-Not-Track Online Act of 2011, S. 913, 112th Congress (2011); Do Not Track Me Online Act, H.R. 654, 112th Congress (2011).

12 *See* Press Release, Microsoft, Providing Windows Customers with More Choice and Control of Their Privacy Online with Internet Explorer 9 (Dec. 7, 2010), *available at* http://www.microsoft.com/presspass/features/2010/dec10/12-07ie9privacyqa. mspx; *Mozilla Firefox 4 Beta, Now Including "Do Not Track" Capabilities*, MOZILLA BLOG (Feb. 8, 2011), http://blog.mozilla. com/blog/2011/02/08/mozilla-firefox-4-beta-now-including-do-not-track-capabilities/; Nick Wingfield, *Apple Adds Do-Not-Track Tool to New Browser*, WALL ST. J., Apr. 13, 2011, *available at* http://online.wsj.com/article/SB1000142405274870355 1304576261272308358858.html. Google recently announced that it will also offer this capability in the next version of its browser. Gregg Kaizer, *FAQ: What Google's Do Not Track Move Means*, COMPUTERWORLD (Feb. 24, 2012), *available at* http:// www.computerworld.com/s/article/9224583/FAQ_What_Google_s_Do_Not_Track_move_means.

13 *See* Mozilla, Do Not Track FAQs, http://dnt.mozilla.org.

14 *See* Press Release, Interactive Advertising Bureau, Major Marketing/Media Trade Groups Launch Program to Give Consumers Enhanced Control Over Collection and Use of Web Viewing Data for Online Behavioral Advertising (Oct. 4, 2010), *available at* http://www.iab.net/about_the_iab/recent_press_releases/press_release_archive/press_release/pr-100410.

Finally, the World Wide Web Consortium ("W3C")[15] convened a working group to create a universal standard for Do Not Track. The working group includes DAA member companies, other U.S. and international companies, industry groups, and consumer groups. The W3C group has made substantial progress toward a standard that is workable in the desktop and mobile settings, and has published two working drafts of its standard documents. The group's goal is to complete a consensus standard in the coming months.

2. OTHER PRIVACY INITIATIVES

Beyond the Do Not Track developments, broader initiatives to improve consumer privacy are underway in Congress, Federal agencies, and the private sector. For example, Congress is considering several general privacy bills that would establish a regulatory framework for protecting consumer privacy by improving transparency about the commercial uses of personal information and providing consumers with choice about such use.[16] The bills would also provide the Commission rulemaking authority concerning, among other things, notice, consent, and the transfer of information to third parties.

In the House of Representatives, Members have introduced bipartisan legislation to amend the Children's Online Privacy Protection Act[17] ("COPPA") and establish other protections for children and teens.[18] The bill would prohibit the collection and use of minors' information for targeted marketing and would require websites to permit the deletion of publicly available information of minors. Members of Congress also introduced a number of other bills addressing data security and data breach notification in 2011.[19]

---

15 The W3C is an international standard-setting body that works "to lead the World Wide Web to its full potential by developing protocols and guidelines that ensure the long-term growth of the Web." *See* W3C Mission, http://www.w3.org/ Consortium/mission.html.

16 *See* Commercial Privacy Bill of Rights Act of 2011, S. 799, 112th Congress (2011); Building Effective Strategies To Promote Responsibility Accountability Choice Transparency Innovation Consumer Expectations and Safeguards Act, H.R. 611, 112th Congress (2011); Consumer Privacy Protection Act of 2011, H.R. 1528, 112th Congress (2011).

17 Children's Online Privacy Protection Act of 1998, 15 U.S.C. §§ 6501-6506.

18 *See* Do Not Track Kids Act of 2011, H.R. 1895, 112th Congress (2011). In September 2011, the Commission issued a Notice of Proposed Rulemaking, proposing changes to the COPPA Rule to address changes in technology. *See FTC Children's Online Privacy Protection Rule*, 76 Fed. Reg. 59804 (proposed Sep. 27, 2011), *available at* http://www.ftc.gov/ os/2011/09/110915coppa.pdf.

19 *See* Personal Data Privacy and Security Act of 2011, S. 1151, 112th Congress (2011); Data Security and Breach Notification Act of 2011, S. 1207, 112th Congress (2011); Data Breach Notification Act of 2011, S.1408, 112th Congress (2011); Data Security Act of 2011, S.1434, 112th Congress (2011); Personal Data Protection and Breach Accountability Act of 2011, S. 1535, 112th Congress (2011); Data Accountability and Trust Act, H.R. 1707, 112th Congress (2011); Data Accountability and Trust Act of 2011, H.R. 1841, 112th Congress (2011); Secure and Fortify Electronic Data Act, H.R. 2577, 112th Congress (2011).

Federal agencies have taken significant steps to improve consumer privacy as well. For its part, since issuing the preliminary staff report, the FTC has resolved seven data security cases,[20] obtained orders against Google, Facebook, and online ad networks,[21] and challenged practices that violate sector-specific privacy laws like the Fair Credit Reporting Act ("FCRA") and COPPA.[22] The Commission has also proposed amendments to the COPPA Rule to address changes in technology. The comment period on the Proposed Rulemaking ran through December 23, 2011, and the Commission is currently reviewing the comments received.[23] Additionally, the Commission has hosted public workshops on discrete privacy issues such as child identity theft and the use of facial recognition technology.

Other federal agencies have also begun examining privacy issues. In 2011, the Federal Communications Commission ("FCC") hosted a public forum to address privacy concerns associated with location-based services.[24] The Department of Health and Human Services ("HHS") hosted a forum on medical identity theft, developed a model privacy notice for personal health records,[25] and is developing legislative recommendations on privacy and security for such personal health records. In addition, HHS recently launched an initiative to identify privacy and security best practices for using mobile devices in health care settings.[26]

---

20 *See In the Matter of Upromise, Inc.,* FTC File No. 102 3116 (Jan. 18, 2012) (proposed consent order), *available at* http://www.ftc.gov/os/caselist/1023116/index.shtm; *In the Matter of ACRAnet, Inc.,* FTC Docket No. C-4331 (Aug. 17, 2011) (consent order), *available at* http://www.ftc.gov/os/caselist/0923088/index.shtm; *In the Matter of SettlementOne Credit Corp.,* FTC Docket No. C-4330 (Aug. 17, 2011) (consent order), *available at* http://www.ftc.gov/os/caselist/0823208/index.shtm; *In the Matter of Ceridian Corp.,* FTC Docket No. C-4325 (June 8, 2011) (consent order), *available at* http://www.ftc.gov/os/caselist/1023160/index.shtm; *In the Matter of Lookout Servs., Inc.,* FTC Docket No. C-4326 (June 15, 2011) (consent order), *available at* http://www.ftc.gov/os/caselist/1023076/index.shtm; *In the Matter of Twitter, Inc.,* FTC Docket No. C-4316 (Mar. 2, 2011) (consent order), *available at* http://www.ftc.gov/os/caselist/0923093/index.shtm; *In the Matter of Fajilan & Assocs., Inc.,* FTC Docket No. C-4332 (Aug. 17, 2011) (consent order), *available at* http://www.ftc.gov/os/caselist/0923089/index.shtm.

21 *See In the Matter of Google, Inc.,* FTC Docket No. C-4336 (Oct. 13, 2011) (consent order), *available at* http://www.ftc.gov/os/caselist/1023136/index.shtm (requiring company to implement privacy program subject to independent third-party audit); *In the Matter of Facebook, Inc.,* FTC File No. 092 3184 (Nov. 29, 2011) (proposed consent order), *available at* http://www.ftc.gov/os/caselist/0923184/index.shtm (requiring company to implement privacy program subject to independent third-party audit); *In the Matter of Chitika, Inc.,* FTC Docket No. C-4324 (June 7, 2011) (consent order), *available at* http://www.ftc.gov/os/caselist/1023087/index.shtm (requiring company's behavioral advertising opt out to last for five years); *In the Matter of ScanScout, Inc.,* FTC Docket No. C-4344 (Dec. 14, 2011) (consent order), *available at* http://www.ftc.gov/os/caselist/1023185/index.shtm (requiring company to improve disclosure of its data collection practices and offer consumers a user-friendly opt out mechanism).

22 Fair Credit Reporting Act, 15 U.S.C. § 1681 *et seq.*; COPPA Rule, 16 C.F.R. Part 312; *see also, e.g., United States v. W3 Innovations, LLC,* No. CV-11-03958 (N.D. Cal. Sept. 8, 2011) (COPPA consent decree); *United States v. Teletrack, Inc.,* No. 1 11-CV-2060 (N.D. Ga. filed June 24, 2011) (FCRA consent decree); *United States v. Playdom, Inc.,* No. SACV-11-00724-AG (ANx) (C.D. Cal. May 24, 2011) (COPPA consent decree).

23 *See* Press Release, FTC Extends Deadline for Comments on Proposed Amendments to the Children's Online Privacy Protection Rule Until December 23 (Nov. 18, 2011), *available at* http://www.ftc.gov/opa/2011/11/coppa.shtm.

24 *See* FCC Workshop, *Helping Consumers Harness the Potential of Location-Based Services* (June 28, 2011), *available at* http://www.fcc.gov/events/location-based-services-forum.

25 *See* The Office of the National Coordinator for Health Information Technology, Personal Health Record (PHR) Model Privacy Notice, http://healthit.hhs.gov/portal/server.pt/community/healthit_hhs_gov__draft_phr_model_notice/1176.

26 *See* HHS Workshop, *Mobile Devices Roundtable: Safeguarding Health Information, available at* http://healthit.hhs.gov/portal/server.pt/community/healthit_hhs_gov__mobile_devices_roundtable/3815.

The private sector has taken steps to enhance user privacy and security as well. For example, Google and Facebook have improved authentication mechanisms to give users stronger protection against compromised passwords.[27] Also, privacy-enhancing technologies such as the HTTPS Everywhere browser add-on have given users additional tools to encrypt their information in transit.[28] On the mobile front, the Mobile Marketing Association released its Mobile Application Privacy Policy.[29] This document provides guidance on privacy principles for application ("app") developers and discusses how to inform consumers about the collection and use of their data. Despite these developments, as explained below, industry still has more work to do to promote consumer privacy.

III. MAIN THEMES FROM COMMENTERS

The more than 450 comments filed in response to the preliminary staff report addressed three overarching issues: how privacy harms should be articulated; the value of global interoperability of different privacy regimes; and the desirability of baseline privacy legislation to augment self-regulatory efforts. Those comments, and the Commission's analysis, are discussed below.

A. ARTICULATION OF PRIVACY HARMS

There was broad consensus among commenters that consumers need basic privacy protections for their personal information. This is true particularly in light of the complexity of the current personal data ecosystem. Some commenters also stated that the Commission should recognize a broader set of privacy harms than those involving physical and economic injury.[30] For example, one commenter cited complaints from consumers who had been surreptitiously tracked and targeted with prescription drug offers and other health-related materials regarding sensitive medical conditions.[31]

At the same time, some commenters questioned whether the costs of broader privacy protections were justified by the anticipated benefits.[32] Relatedly, many commenters raised concerns about how wider privacy protections would affect innovation and the ability to offer consumers beneficial new products and services.[33]

---

27   *See Advanced Sign-In Security For Your Google Account*, GOOGLE OFFICIAL BLOG (Feb. 10, 2011, 11:30 AM), http://googleblog.blogspot.com/2011/02/advanced-sign-in-security-for-your.html#!/2011/02/advanced-sign-in-security-for-your.html; Andrew Song, *Introducing Login Approvals*, FACEBOOK BLOG (May 12, 2011, 9:58 AM), http://www.facebook.com/note.php?note_id=10150172618258920.

28   *See HTTPS Everywhere*, ELECTRONIC FRONTIER FOUNDATION, https://www.eff.org/https-everywhere.

29   *See* Press Release, Mobile Marketing Association, Mobile Marketing Association Releases Final Privacy Policy Guidelines for Mobile Apps (Jan. 25, 2012), *available at* http://mmaglobal.com/news/mobile-marketing-association -releases-final-privacy-policy-guidelines-mobile-apps.

30   *See Comment of TRUSTe*, cmt. #00450, at 3; *Comment of Berlin Commissioner for Data Protection & Freedom of Information*, cmt. #00484, at 1.

31   *See Comment of Patient Privacy Rights*, cmt. #00470, at 2.

32   *See Comment of Technology Policy Institute*, cmt. #00301, at 5-8; *Comment of Experian*, cmt. #00398, at 9-11; *Comment of Global Privacy Alliance*, cmt. #00367, at 6-7.

33   *See Comment of Facebook, Inc.*, cmt. #00413, at 1-2, 7-8; *Comment of Google, Inc.*, cmt. #00417, at 4; *Comment of Global Privacy Alliance*, cmt. #00367, at 16.

The Commission agrees that the range of privacy-related harms is more expansive than economic or physical harm or unwarranted intrusions and that any privacy framework should recognize additional harms that might arise from unanticipated uses of data. These harms may include the unexpected revelation of previously private information, including both sensitive information (*e.g.*, health information, precise geolocation information) and less sensitive information (*e.g.*, purchase history, employment history) to unauthorized third parties.[34] As one example, in the Commission's case against Google, the complaint alleged that Google used the information of consumers who signed up for Gmail to populate a new social network, Google Buzz.[35] The creation of that social network in some cases revealed previously private information about Gmail users' most frequent email contacts. Similarly, the Commission's complaint against Facebook alleged that Facebook's sharing of users' personal information beyond their privacy settings was harmful.[36] Like these enforcement actions, a privacy framework should address practices that unexpectedly reveal previously private information even absent physical or financial harm, or unwarranted intrusions.[37]

In terms of weighing costs and benefits, although it recognizes that imposing new privacy protections will not be costless, the Commission believes doing so not only will help consumers but also will benefit businesses by building consumer trust in the marketplace. Businesses frequently acknowledge the importance of consumer trust to the growth of digital commerce[38] and surveys support this view. For

---

34 One former FTC Chairman, in analyzing a spyware case, emphasized that consumers should have control over what is on their computers. Chairman Majoras issued the following statement in connection with the Commission's settlement against Sony BMG resolving claims about the company's installation of invasive tracking software: "Consumers' computers belong to them, and companies must adequately disclose unexpected limitations on the customary use of their products so consumers can make informed decisions regarding whether to purchase and install that content." Press Release, FTC, Sony BMG Settles FTC Charges (Jan. 30, 2007), *available at* http://www.ftc.gov/opa/2007/01/sony.shtm; *see also* Walt Mossberg, *Despite Others' Claims, Tracking Cookies Fit My Spyware Definition*, ALLTHINGSD (July 14, 2005, 12:01 AM), http://allthingsd. com/20050714/tracking-cookies/ ("Suppose you bought a TV set that included a component to track what you watched, and then reported that data back to a company that used or sold it for advertising purposes. Only nobody told you the tracking technology was there or asked your permission to use it. You would likely be outraged at this violation of privacy. Yet that kind of Big Brother intrusion goes on everyday on the Internet . . . [with tracking cookies].").

35 *See In re Google Inc.*, FTC Docket No. C-4336 (Oct. 13, 2011) (consent order), *available at* http://www.ftc.gov/os/caselist/10 23136/110330googlebuzzcompt.pdf.

36 *See In re Facebook, Inc.*, FTC File No. 092 3184 (Nov. 29, 2011) (proposed consent order), *available at* http://www.ftc.gov/os/ caselist/0923184/111129facebookagree.pdf.

37 Although the complaint against Google alleged that the company used deceptive tactics and violated its own privacy promises when it launched Google Buzz, even in the absence of such misrepresentations, revealing previously-private consumer data could cause consumer harm. *See* Press Release, FTC, FTC Charges Deceptive Privacy Practices in Google's Rollout of its Buzz Social Network (Mar. 30, 2011), *available at* http://www.ftc.gov/opa/2011/03/google.shtm (noting that in response to the Buzz launch, Google received thousands of complaints from consumers who were concerned about public disclosure of their email contacts which included, in some cases, ex-spouses, patients, students, employers, or competitors).

38 *See, e.g.*, Statement of John M. Montgomery, GroupM Interaction, *The State of Online Consumer Privacy: Hearing Before the S. Comm. on Commerce, Sci., and Transp.*, 112th Cong. (Mar. 16, 2011), *available at* http://www.iab.net/media/file/ DC1DOCS1-432016-v1-John_Montgomery_-_Written_Testimony.pdf ("We at GroupM strongly believe in protecting consumer privacy. It is not only the right thing to do, but it is also good for business."); Statement of Alan Davidson, Director of Public Policy, Google Inc., *Protecting Mobile Privacy: Your Smartphones, Tablets, Cell Phones and Your Privacy: Hearing Before the S. Subcomm. on Privacy, Tech., and the Law*, 112th Cong. (May 10, 2011), *available at* http://www. judiciary.senate.gov/pdf/11-5-10%20Davidson%20Testimony.pdf ("Protecting privacy and security is essential for Internet commerce.").

example, in the online behavioral advertising area, a recent survey shows that consumers feel better about brands that give them transparency and control over advertisements.[39]

Companies offering consumers information about behavioral advertising and the tools to opt out of it have also found increased customer engagement. In its comment, Google noted that visitors to its Ads Preference Manager are far more likely to edit their interest settings and remain opted in rather than to opt out.[40] Similarly, another commenter conducted a study showing that making its customers aware of its privacy and data security principles – including restricting the sharing of customer data, increasing the transparency of data practices, and providing access to the consumer data it maintains – significantly increased customer trust in its company.[41]

In addition, some companies appear to be competing on privacy. For example, one company offers an Internet search service that it promotes as being far more privacy-sensitive than other search engines.[42] Similarly, in response to Google's decision to change its privacy policies to allow tracking of consumers across different Google products, Microsoft encouraged consumers to switch to Microsoft's more privacy-protective products and services.[43]

The privacy framework is designed to be flexible to permit and encourage innovation. Companies can implement the privacy protections of the framework in a way that is proportional to the nature, sensitivity, and amount of data collected as well as to the size of the business at issue. For example, the framework does not include rigid provisions such as specific disclosures or mandatory data retention and destruction periods. And, as discussed below, the framework streamlines communications for businesses and consumers alike by requiring consumer choice mechanisms only for data practices that are inconsistent with the context of a particular transaction or the business relationship with the consumer.[44]

B. GLOBAL INTEROPERABILITY

Reflecting differing legal, policy, and constitutional regimes, privacy frameworks around the world vary considerably. Many commenters cited the value to both consumers and businesses of promoting more consistent and interoperable approaches to protecting consumer privacy internationally. These commenters stated that consistency between different privacy regimes reduces companies' costs, promotes international competitiveness, and increases compliance with privacy standards.[45]

---

39 *See RESEARCH: Consumers Feel Better About Brands That Give Them Transparency and Control Over Ads*, EVIDON BLOG (Nov. 10, 2010), http://blog.evidon.com/tag/better-advertising ("when advertisers empower consumers with information and control over the ads they receive, a majority feels more positive toward those brands, and 36% even become more likely to purchase from those brands").

40 *See Comment of Google Inc.*, cmt. #00417, at 4.

41 *See Comment of Intuit, Inc.*, cmt. #00348, at 6-8 ("The more transparent (meaning open, simple and clear) the company is, the more customer trust increases. . . .").

42 *See* DuckDuckGo, Privacy Policy, https://duckduckgo.com/privacy.html.

43 *See* Frank X. Shaw, *Gone Google? Got Concerns? We Have Alternatives*, THE OFFICIAL MICROSOFT BLOG (Feb. 1, 2012, 2:00 AM), http://blogs.technet.com/b/microsoft_blog/archive/2012/02/01/gone-google-got-concerns-we-have-alternatives.aspx.

44 See *infra* at Section IV.C.1.a.

45 *See Comment of AT&T Inc.*, cmt. #00420, at 12-13; *Comment of IBM*, cmt. #00433, at 2; *see also Comment of General Electric*, cmt. #00392, at 3 (encouraging international harmonization).

The Commission agrees there is value in greater interoperability among data privacy regimes as consumer data is increasingly transferred around the world. Meaningful protection for such data requires convergence on core principles, an ability of legal regimes to work together, and enhanced cross-border enforcement cooperation. Such interoperability is better for consumers, whose data will be subject to more consistent protection wherever it travels, and more efficient for businesses by reducing the burdens of compliance with differing, and sometimes conflicting, rules. In short, as the Administration White Paper notes, global interoperability "will provide more consistent protections for consumers and lower compliance burdens for companies."[46]

Efforts underway around the world to re-examine current approaches to protecting consumer privacy indicate an interest in convergence on overarching principles and a desire to develop greater interoperability. For example, the Commission's privacy framework is consistent with the nine privacy principles set forth in the 2004 Asia-Pacific Economic Cooperation ("APEC") Privacy Framework. Those principles form the basis for ongoing APEC work to implement a cross-border privacy rules system to facilitate data transfers among the 21 APEC member economies, including the United States.[47] In 2011, the Organization for Economic Cooperation and Development ("OECD") issued a report re-examining its seminal 1980 Privacy Guidelines in light of technological changes over the past thirty years.[48] Further, the European Commission has recently proposed legislation updating its 1995 data protection directive and proposed an overhaul of the European Union approach that focuses on many of the issues raised elsewhere in this report as well as issues relating to international transfers and interoperability.[49] These efforts reflect a commitment to many of the high-level principles embodied in the FTC's framework – increased transparency and consumer control, the need for privacy protections to be built into basic business practices, and the importance of accountability and enforcement. They also reflect a shared international interest in having systems that work better with each other, and are thus better for consumers.

---

46 White House, *Consumer Data Privacy in a Networked World: A Framework for Protecting Privacy and Promoting Innovation in the Global Digital Economy*, ii, Foreword (Feb. 2012), *available at* http://www.whitehouse.gov/sites/default/files/privacy-final. pdf.

47 The nine principles in the APEC Privacy Framework are preventing harm, notice, collection limitations, uses of personal information, choice, integrity of personal information, security safeguards, access and correction, accountability. Businesses have developed a code of conduct based on these nine principles and will obtain third-party certification of their compliance. A network of privacy enforcement authorities from participating APEC economies, such as the FTC, will be able to take enforcement actions against companies that violate their commitments under the code of conduct. *See* Press Release, FTC, FTC Welcomes a New Privacy System for the Movement of Consumer Data Between the United States and Other Economies in the Asia-Pacific Region (Nov. 14, 2011), *available at* http://www.ftc.gov/opa/2011/11/apec.shtm).

48 *See* Organization for Economic Co-operation and Development, *The Evolving Privacy Landscape: 30 Years after the OECD Privacy Guidelines* (Apr. 2011), *available at* http://www.oecd.org/dataoecd/22/25/47683378.pdf.

49 European Commission, *Proposal for a REGULATION OF THE EUROPEAN PARLIAMENT AND OF THE COUNCIL on the protection of individuals with regard to the processing of personal data and on the free movement of such data (General Data Protection Regulation)* (Jan. 25, 2012), *available at* http://ec.europa.eu/justice/data-protection/document/review2012/ com_2012_11_en.pdf.

C. LEGISLATION TO AUGMENT SELF-REGULATORY EFFORTS

Numerous comments, including those from large industry stakeholders, consumer and privacy advocates, and individual consumers supported some form of baseline privacy legislation that incorporates the FIPPs.[50] Business commenters noted that legislation would help provide legal certainty,[51] serve as a key mechanism for building trust among customers,[52] and provide a way to fill gaps in existing sector-based laws.[53] Consumer and privacy advocates cited the inability of self-regulation to provide comprehensive and long-lasting protection for consumers.[54] One such commenter cited the fact that many self-regulatory initiatives that arose in response to the Commission's 2000 recommendation for privacy legislation were short-lived and failed to provide long-term privacy protections for consumers.[55]

At the same time, a number of commenters raised concerns about government action beyond providing guidance for self-regulatory programs.[56] Some cautioned the FTC about taking an approach that might impede industry's ability to innovate and develop new products and services in a rapidly changing marketplace. Others noted that a regulatory approach could lead to picking "winners and losers" among particular technologies and business models and called for a technology-neutral approach.[57] Commenters also argued that it might be impractical to craft omnibus standards or rules that would apply broadly across different business sectors.[58]

The Commission agrees that, to date, self-regulation has not gone far enough. In most areas, with the notable exception of efforts surrounding Do Not Track, there has been little self-regulation. For example, the FTC's recent survey of mobile apps marketed to children revealed that many of these apps fail to provide any disclosure about the extent to which they collect and share consumers' personal data.[59] Similarly, efforts

---

50 *See, e.g., Comment of eBay*, cmt. #00374, at 2; *Comment of Intel Corp.*, cmt. #00246, at 3-7; *Comment of Microsoft Corp.*, cmt. #00395, at 4; *Comment of Intuit, Inc.*, cmt. #00348, at 13-14; *Comment of Center for Democracy & Technology*, cmt. #00469, at 1, 7; *Comment of Gregory Byrd*, cmt. #00144, at 1; *Comment of Ellen Klinefelter*, cmt. #00095, at 1.

51 *See Comment of Microsoft Corp.*, cmt. #00395, at 4.

52 *See Comment of Intel Corp.*, cmt. #00246, at 3.

53 *See Comment of Intuit, Inc.*, cmt. #00348, at 13.

54 *See Comment of Electronic Privacy Information Center*, cmt. #00386, at 2; *Comment of World Privacy Forum*, cmt. #00376, at 2-3, 8-17.

55 *See Comment of World Privacy Forum*, cmt. #00376, at 2-3, 8-17.

56 *See Comment of Consumer Data Industry Ass'n*, cmt. #00363, at 4-5; *Comment of American Catalog Mailers Ass'n*, cmt. #00424, at 3; *Comment of Facebook, Inc.*, cmt. #00413, at 13-14; *Comment of Google Inc.*, cmt. #00417, at 8; *Comment of Verizon*, cmt. #00428, at 2-3, 6-7, 14-17; *Comment of Mortgage Bankers Ass'n*, cmt. #00308, at 2; *Comment of National Cable & Telecommunications Ass'n*, cmt. #00432, at 3, 5, 7-13; *Comment of CTIA – The Wireless Ass'n*, cmt. #00375, at 15.

57 *See Comment of National Cable & Telecommunications Ass'n*, cmt. #00432, at 32-37; *Comment of USTelecom*, cmt. #00411, at 5-7; *Comment of Verizon*, cmt. #00428, at 4-6; *Comment of Direct Marketing Ass'n, Inc.*, cmt. #00449, at 5-6.

58 *See Comment of Consumer Data Industry Ass'n*, cmt. #00363, at 4-6; *see also Comment of CTIA - The Wireless Ass'n*, cmt. #00375, at 8-11; *Comment of Direct Marketing Ass'n, Inc.*, cmt. #00449, at 13.

59 FTC Staff, *Mobile Apps for Kids: Current Privacy Disclosures are Disappointing* (Feb. 2012), *available at* http://www.ftc.gov/os/2012/02/120216mobile_apps_kids.pdf; *FPF Finds Nearly Three-Quarters of Most Downloaded Mobile Apps Lack a Privacy Policy*, FUTURE OF PRIVACY FORUM, http://www.futureofprivacy.org/2011/05/12/fpf-finds-nearly-three-quarters-of-most-downloaded-mobile-apps-lack-a-privacy-policy/.

of the data broker industry to establish self-regulatory rules concerning consumer privacy have fallen short.[60] These examples illustrate that even in some well-established markets, basic privacy concepts like transparency about the nature of companies' data practices and meaningful consumer control are absent. This absence erodes consumer trust.

There is also widespread evidence of data breaches and vulnerabilities related to consumer information.[61] Published reports indicate that some breaches may have resulted from the unintentional release of consumer data, for which companies later apologized and took action to address.[62] Other incidents involved planned releases or uses of data by companies that ultimately did not occur due to consumer and public backlash.[63] Still other incidents involved companies' failure to take reasonable precautions and resulted in FTC consent decrees. These incidents further undermine consumer trust, which is essential for business growth and innovation.[64]

The ongoing and widespread incidents of unauthorized or improper use and sharing of personal information are evidence of two points. First, companies that do not intend to undermine consumer privacy simply lack sufficiently clear standards to operate and innovate while respecting the expectations of consumers. Second, companies that do seek to cut corners on consumer privacy do not have adequate legal incentives to curtail such behavior.

To provide clear standards and appropriate incentives to ensure basic privacy protections across all industry sectors, in addition to reiterating its call for federal data security legislation,[65] the Commission calls

---

60   *See Comment of Center for Democracy & Technology*, cmt. #00469, at 2-3; *Comment of World Privacy Forum*, cmt. #00376, at 2-3. Discussed more fully *infra* at Section IV.D.2.a.

61   *See* Grant Gross, *Lawmakers Question Sony, Epsilon on Data Breaches,* PC World (June 2, 2011 3:40 PM), *available at* http://www.pcworld.com/businesscenter/article/229258/lawmakers_question_sony_epsilon_on_data_breaches.html; Dwight Silverman, *App Privacy: Who's Uploading Your Contact List?*, Houston Chronicle (Feb. 15, 2012 8:10 AM), http://blog.chron.com/techblog/2012/02/app-privacy-whos-uploading-your-contact-list/; Dan Graziano, *Like iOS apps, Android Apps Can Secretly Access Photos Thanks to Loophole,* BGR (Mar. 1, 2012 3:45 PM), http://www.bgr.com/2012/03/01/like-ios-apps-android-apps-can-also-secretly-access-photos-thanks-to-security-hole/.

62   *CEO Apologizes After Path Social App Uploads Contact Lists,* KMOV.com (Feb. 9, 2012 11:11AM), http://www.kmov.com/news/consumer/CEO-apologizes-after-Path-uploads-contact-lists--139015729.html; Daisuke Wakabayashi, *A Contrite Sony Vows Tighter Security,* Wall St. J. May 1, 2011, *available at* http://online.wsj.com/article/SB10001424052748704436004576296302384608280.html.

63   Kevin Parrish, *OnStar Changes its Mind About Tracking Vehicles,* Tom's Guide (Sept. 29, 2011 7:30 AM), http://www.tomsguide.com/us/OnStar-General-motors-Linda-Marshall-GPS-Terms-and-conditions,news-12677.html.

64   Surveys of consumer attitudes towards privacy conducted in the past year are illuminating. For example, a *USA Today*/Gallup poll indicated that a majority of the Facebook members or Google users surveyed were "very" or "somewhat concerned" about their privacy while using these services. Lymari Morales, *Google and Facebook Users Skew Young, Affluent, and Educated,* Gallup (Feb. 17, 2011), *available at* http://www.gallup.com/poll/146159/facebook-google-users-skew-young-affluent-educated.aspx.

65   The Commission has long supported federal laws requiring companies to implement reasonable security measures and to notify consumers in the event of certain security breaches. *See, e.g.*, Prepared Statement of the FTC, *Data Security: Hearing Before the H. Comm. on Energy and Commerce, Subcomm. on Commerce, Manufacturing, and Trade*, 112th Cong. (June 15, 2011), *available at* http://www.ftc.gov/os/testimony/110615datasecurityhouse.pdf; Prepared Statement of the FTC, *Protecting Social Security Numbers From Identity Theft: Hearing Before the Before the H. Comm. on Ways and Means, Subcomm. on Social Security*, 112th Cong. (April 13, 2011), *available at* http://www.ftc.gov/os/testimony/110411ssn-idtheft.pdf; FTC, *Security in Numbers, SSNs and ID Theft* (Dec. 2008), *available at* http://www.ftc.gov/os/2008/12/P075414ssnreport.pdf; President's Identity Theft Task Force, *Identity Theft Task Force Report* (Sept. 2008), *available at* http://www.idtheft.gov/reports/IDTReport2008.pdf.

on Congress to consider enacting baseline privacy legislation that is technologically neutral and sufficiently flexible to allow companies to continue to innovate. The Commission is prepared to work with Congress and other stakeholders to craft such legislation.

In their comments, many businesses indicated that they already incorporate the FIPPS into their practices. For these companies, a legislative mandate should not impose an undue burden and indeed, will "level the playing field" by ensuring that all companies are required to incorporate these principles into their practices.

For those companies that are not already taking consumer privacy into account – either because of lack of understanding or lack of concern – legislation should provide clear rules of the road. It should also provide adequate deterrence through the availability of civil penalties and other remedies.[66] In short, legislation will provide businesses with the certainty they need to understand their obligations and the incentive to meet those obligations, while providing consumers with confidence that businesses will be required to respect their privacy. This approach will create an environment that allows businesses to continue to innovate and consumers to embrace those innovations without sacrificing their privacy.[67] The Commission is prepared to work with Congress and other stakeholders to formulate baseline privacy legislation.

While Congress considers such legislation, the Commission urges industry to accelerate the pace of its self-regulatory measures to implement the Commission's final privacy framework. Over the course of the next year, Commission staff will promote the framework's implementation by focusing its policymaking efforts on five main action items, which are highlighted here and discussed further throughout the report.

- ◆ **Do Not Track:** As discussed above, industry has made significant progress in implementing Do Not Track. The browser vendors have developed tools that consumers can use to signal that they do not want to be tracked; the DAA has developed its own icon-based tool and has committed to honor the browser tools; and the W3C has made substantial progress in creating an international standard for Do Not Track. However, the work is not done. The Commission will work with these groups to complete implementation of an easy-to use, persistent, and effective Do Not Track system.

- ◆ **Mobile:** The Commission calls on companies providing mobile services to work toward improved privacy protections, including the development of short, meaningful disclosures. To this end, FTC staff has initiated a project to update its business guidance about online advertising disclosures.[68] As part of this project, staff will host a workshop on May 30, 2012 and will address, among other issues, mobile privacy disclosures and how these disclosures can be short, effective, and accessible to

---

66 Former FTC Chairman Casper "Cap" Weinberger recognized the value of civil penalties as a deterrent to unlawful conduct. *See Hearings on H.R. 14931 and Related Bills before the Subcomm. on Commerce and Finance of the H. Comm. on Interstate and Foreign Commerce*, 91st Cong. 53, 54 (1970) (statement of FTC Chairman Caspar Weinberger); *Hearings on S. 2246, S. 3092, and S. 3201 Before the Consumer Subcomm. of the S. Comm. on Commerce*, 91st Cong. 9 (1970) (Letter from FTC Chairman Caspar W. Weinberger) (forwarding copy of House testimony).

67 With this report, the Commission is not seeking to impose civil penalties for privacy violations under the FTC Act. Rather, in the event Congress enacts privacy legislation, the Commission believes that such legislation would be more effective if the FTC were authorized to obtain civil penalties for violations.

68 *See* Press Release, FTC, FTC Seeks Input to Revising its Guidance to Businesses About Disclosures in Online Advertising (May 26, 2011), *available at* http://www.ftc.gov/opa/2011/05/dotcom.shtm.

consumers on small screens. The Commission hopes that the workshop will spur further industry self-regulation in this area.

♦ **Data Brokers:** To address the invisibility of, and consumers' lack of control over, data brokers' collection and use of consumer information, the Commission supports targeted legislation – similar to that contained in several of the data security bills introduced in the 112th Congress – that would provide consumers with access to information about them held by a data broker.[69] To further increase transparency, the Commission calls on data brokers that compile data for marketing purposes to explore creating a centralized website where data brokers could (1) identify themselves to consumers and describe how they collect and use consumer data and (2) detail the access rights and other choices they provide with respect to the consumer data they maintain.

♦ **Large Platform Providers:** To the extent that large platforms, such as Internet Service Providers ("ISPs"), operating systems, browsers, and social media, seek to comprehensively track consumers' online activities, it raises heightened privacy concerns. To further explore privacy and other issues related to this type of comprehensive tracking, FTC staff intends to host a public workshop in the second half of 2012.

♦ **Promoting enforceable self-regulatory codes:** The Department of Commerce, with the support of key industry stakeholders, is undertaking a project to facilitate the development of sector-specific codes of conduct. FTC staff will participate in that project. To the extent that strong privacy codes are developed, the Commission will view adherence to such codes favorably in connection with its law enforcement work. The Commission will also continue to enforce the FTC Act to take action against companies that engage in unfair or deceptive practices, including the failure to abide by self-regulatory programs they join.

---

69 *See* Data Accountability and Trust Act, H.R. 1707, 112th Congress (2011); Data Accountability and Trust Act of 2011, H.R. 1841, 112th Congress (2011); Data Security and Breach Notification Act of 2011, S. 1207, 112th Congress (2011).

IV. PRIVACY FRAMEWORK

In addition to the general comments described above, the Commission received significant comments on the scope of the proposed framework and each individual element. Those comments, as well as several clarifications and refinements based on the Commission's analysis of the issues raised, are discussed below.

A. SCOPE

> **Proposed Scope:** The framework applies to all commercial entities that collect or use consumer data that can be reasonably linked to a specific consumer, computer, or other device.

A variety of commenters addressed the framework's proposed scope. Some of these commenters supported an expansive reach while others proposed limiting the framework's application to particular types of entities and carving out certain categories of businesses. Commenters also called for further clarification regarding the type of data the framework covers and staff's proposed "reasonably linked" standard.

1. COMPANIES SHOULD COMPLY WITH THE FRAMEWORK UNLESS THEY HANDLE ONLY LIMITED AMOUNTS OF NON-SENSITIVE DATA THAT IS NOT SHARED WITH THIRD PARTIES.

Numerous commenters addressed whether the framework should apply to entities that collect, maintain, or use limited amounts of data. Several companies argued that the burden the framework could impose on small businesses outweighed the reduced risk of harm from the collection and use of limited amounts of non-sensitive consumer data.[70] These commenters proposed that the framework not apply to entities that collect or use non-sensitive data from fewer than 5,000 individuals a year where the data is used for limited purposes, such as internal operations and first-party marketing.[71] As additional support for this position, these commenters noted that proposed privacy legislation introduced in the 111th Congress contained an exclusion to this effect.[72]

Although one consumer and privacy organization supported a similar exclusion,[73] others expressed concern about exempting, *per se*, any types of businesses or quantities of data from the framework's scope.[74] These commenters pointed to the possibility that excluded companies would sell the data to third parties, such as advertising networks or data brokers.

The Commission agrees that the first-party collection and use of non-sensitive data (*e.g.*, data that is not a Social Security number or financial, health, children's, or geolocation information) creates fewer privacy

---

70   *See Comment of eBay, Inc.*, cmt. #00374, at 3; *Comment of Microsoft Corp.*, cmt. #00395, at 4.

71   *Id.*

72   *See* BEST PRACTICES ACT, H.R. 5777, 111th Congress (2010); Staff Discussion Draft, H.R. __ , 111th Congress (2010), *available at* http://www.nciss.org/legislation/BoucherStearnsprivacydiscussiondraft.pdf.

73   *Comment of the Center for Democracy & Technology*, cmt. #00469, at 1.

74   *See Comment of the Electronic Frontier Foundation*, cmt. #00400, at 1; *Comment of the Consumer Federation of America*, cmt. #00358, at 2.

concerns than practices that involve sensitive data or sharing with third parties.[75] Accordingly, entities that collect limited amounts of non-sensitive consumer data from under 5,000 consumers need not comply with the framework, as long as they do not share the data with third parties. For example, consider a cash-only curb-side food truck business that offers to send messages announcing when it is in a given neighborhood to consumers who provide their email addresses. As long as the food truck business does not share these email addresses with third parties, the Commission believes that it need not provide privacy disclosures to its customers. This narrow exclusion acknowledges the need for flexibility for businesses that collect limited amounts of non-sensitive information. It also recognizes that some business practices create fewer potential risks to consumer information.

2. THE FRAMEWORK SETS FORTH BEST PRACTICES AND CAN WORK IN TANDEM WITH EXISTING PRIVACY AND SECURITY STATUTES.

The proposed framework's applicability to commercial sectors that are covered by existing laws generated comments primarily from representatives of the healthcare and financial services industries. These commenters noted that statutes such as the Health Insurance Portability and Accountability Act ("HIPAA"), the Health Information Technology for Economic and Clinical Health Act ("HITECH"), and the Gramm-Leach-Bliley Act ("GLBA") already impose privacy protections and security requirements through legal obligations on companies in these industries.[76] Accordingly, these commenters urged the Commission to avoid creating duplicative or inconsistent standards and to clarify that the proposed framework is intended to cover only those entities that are not currently covered by existing privacy and security laws. Another commenter, however, urged government to focus on fulfilling consumer privacy expectations across all sectors, noting that market evolution is blurring distinctions about who is covered by HIPAA and that consumers expect organizations to protect their personal health information, regardless of any sector-specific boundaries.[77]

The Commission recognizes the concern regarding potentially inconsistent privacy obligations and notes that, to the extent Congress enacts any of the Commission's recommendations through legislation, such legislation should not impose overlapping or duplicative requirements on conduct that is already regulated.[78] However, the framework is meant to encourage best practices and is not intended to conflict with requirements of existing laws and regulations. To the extent that components of the framework exceed, but do not conflict with existing statutory requirements, entities covered by those statutes should view the framework as best practices to promote consumer privacy. For example, it may be appropriate for financial institutions covered by GLBA to incorporate elements of privacy by design, such as collection limitations, or

---

75 See *infra* at Sections IV.C.1.b.(v) and IV.C.2.e.(ii), for a discussion of what constitutes sensitive data.

76 *See Comment of the Confidentiality Coalition c/o the Healthcare Leadership Council*, cmt. #00349, at 1-4; *Comment of Experian*, cmt. #00398, at 8-10; *Comment of IMS Health*, cmt. #00380, at 2-3; *Comment of Medco Health Solutions, Inc.*, cmt. #00393, at 3; *Comment of SIFMA*, cmt. #00265, at 2-3.

77 *Comment of The Markle Foundation*, cmt. #00456, at 3-10.

78 Any baseline privacy law Congress may enact would likely consider the best way to take into account obligations under existing statutes.

to improve transparency by providing reasonable access to consumer data in a manner that does not conflict with their statutory obligations. In any event, the framework provides an important baseline for entities that are not subject to sector-specific laws like HIPAA or GLBA.[79]

3. THE FRAMEWORK APPLIES TO OFFLINE AS WELL AS ONLINE DATA.

In addressing the framework's applicability to "all commercial entities," numerous commenters discussed whether the framework should apply to both online and offline data. Diverse commenters expressed strong support for a comprehensive approach applicable to both online and offline data practices.[80] Commenters noted that as a practical matter, many companies collect both online and offline data.[81]

Commenters also listed different offline contexts in which entities collect consumer data. These include instances where a consumer interacts directly with a business, such as through the use of a retail loyalty card, or where a non-consumer facing entity, such as a data broker, obtains consumer data from an offline third-party source.[82] One commenter noted that, regardless of whether an entity collects or uses data from an online or an offline source, consumer privacy interests are equally affected.[83] To emphasize the importance of offline data protections, this commenter noted that while the behavioral advertising industry has started to implement self-regulatory measures to improve consumers' ability to control the collection and the use of their online data, in the offline context such efforts by data brokers and others have largely failed.[84]

By contrast, a financial industry organization argued that the FTC should take a more narrow approach by limiting the scope of the proposed framework in a number of respects, including its applicability to offline data collection and use.[85] This commenter stated that some harms in the online context may not exist offline and raised concern about the framework's unintended consequences. For example, the commenter cited the significant costs that a requirement to provide consumers with access to data collected about them

---

79   There may be entities that operate within covered sectors but that nevertheless fall outside of a specific law's scope. For instance, a number of entities that collect health information are not subject to HIPAA. These entities include providers of personal health records – online portfolios that consumers can use to store and keep track of their medical information. In 2009, Congress passed the HITECH Act, which required HHS, in consultation with the FTC, to develop legislative recommendations on privacy and security requirements that should apply to these providers of personal health records and related entities. Health Information Technology ("HITECH") Provisions of American Recovery and Reinvestment Act of 2009, Title XIII, Subtitle D (Pub. L. 111-5, 123 Stat. 115, codified in relevant part at 42 U.S.C. §§ 17937 and 17954). FTC staff is consulting with HHS on this project.

80   *See Comment of the Center for Democracy & Technology*, cmt. #00469, at 2; *Comment of the Computer & Communications Industry Ass'n*, cmt. #00434, at 14; *Comment of Consumers Union*, cmt. #00362, at 4-5; *Comment of the Department of Veterans Affairs*, cmt. #00479, at 3; *Comment of Experian*, cmt. #00398, at 1; *Comment of Google Inc.*, cmt. #00417, at 7; *Comment of Microsoft Corp.*, cmt. #00395, at 4.

81   *See Comment of the Department of Veterans Affairs*, cmt. #00479, at 3 n.7; *Comment of the Computer & Communications Industry Ass'n*, cmt. #00434, at 14; *Comment of Consumers Union*, cmt. #00362, at 1.

82   *See Comment of the Department of Veterans Affairs*, cmt. #00479, at 3 n.7; *Comment of the Computer & Communications Industry Ass'n*, cmt. #00434, at 14.

83   *Comment of Center for Democracy & Technology*, cmt. #00469, at 2.

84   *Comment of Center for Democracy & Technology*, cmt. #00469, at 2-3.

85   *Comment of the Financial Services Forum*, cmt. #00381, at 8-9.

would impose on companies that collect and maintain data in paper rather than electronic form. Another commenter cited the costs of providing privacy disclosures and choices in an offline environment.[86]

The Commission notes that consumers face a landscape of virtually ubiquitous collection of their data. Whether such collection occurs online or offline does not alter the consumer's privacy interest in his or her data. For example, the sale of a consumer profile containing the consumer's purchase history from a brick-and-mortar pharmacy or a bookstore would not implicate fewer privacy concerns simply because the profile contains purchases from an offline retailer rather than from an online merchant. Accordingly, the framework applies in all commercial contexts, both online and offline.

4. THE FRAMEWORK APPLIES TO DATA THAT IS REASONABLY LINKABLE TO A SPECIFIC CONSUMER, COMPUTER, OR DEVICE.

The scope issue that generated the most comments, from a wide range of interested parties, was the proposed framework's applicability to "consumer data that can be reasonably linked to a specific consumer, computer, or other device."

A number of commenters supported the proposed framework's application to data that, while not traditionally considered personally identifiable, is linkable to a consumer or device. In particular, several consumer and privacy groups elaborated on the privacy concerns associated with supposedly anonymous data and discussed the decreasing relevance of the personally identifiable information ("PII") label.[87] These commenters pointed to studies demonstrating consumers' objections to being tracked, regardless of whether the tracker explicitly learns a consumer name, and the potential for harm, such as discriminatory pricing based on online browsing history, even without the use of PII.[88]

Similarly, the commenters noted, the ability to re-identify "anonymous" data supports the proposed framework's application to data that can be reasonably linked to a consumer or device. They pointed to incidents, identified in the preliminary staff report, in which individuals were re-identified from publicly released data sets that did not contain PII.[89] One commenter pointed out that certain industries extensively

---

86 *Comment of National Retail Federation*, cmt. #00419, at 6 (urging FTC to limit privacy framework to online collection of consumer data because applying it to offline collection would be onerous for businesses and consumers).

87 *See Comment of the Center for Democracy & Technology*, cmt. #00469, at 3; *Comment of Consumers Union*, cmt. #00362, at 4-5. In addition, in their comments both AT&T and Mozilla recognized that the distinction between PII and non-PII is blurring. *Comment of AT&T Inc.*, cmt. #00420, at 13; *Comment of Mozilla*, cmt. #00480, at 6.

88 *Comment of Center for Democracy & Technology*, cmt. #00469, at 3 (citing Edward C. Baig, *Internet Users Say, Don't Track Me*, USA TODAY, Dec. 14, 2010, *available at* http://www.usatoday.com/money/advertising/2010-12-14-donottrackpoll14_ ST_N.htm); Scott Cleland, *Americans Want Online Privacy – Per New Zogby Poll*, THE PRECURSOR BLOG (June 8, 2010), http://www.precursorblog.com/content/americans-want-online-privacy-new-zogby-poll); *Comment of Consumers Union*, cmt. #00362, at 4 (discussing the potential for discriminatory pricing (citing Annie Lowery, *How Online Retailers Stay a Step Ahead of Comparison Shoppers*, WASH. POST, Dec. 12, 2010, *available at* http://www.washingtonpost.com/wp-dyn/content/ article/2010/12/11/AR2010121102435.html)).

89 For a brief discussion of such incidents, see FTC, *Protecting Consumer Privacy in an Era of Rapid Change, A Proposed Framework for Businesses and Policymakers, Preliminary FTC Staff Report*, at 38 (Dec. 2010), *available at* http://www.ftc.gov/ os/2010/12/101201privacyreport.pdf.

mine data for marketing purposes and that re-identification is a commercial enterprise.[90] This adds to the likelihood of data re-identification.

Some industry commenters also recognized consumers' privacy interest in data that goes beyond what is strictly labeled PII.[91] Drawing on the FTC's roundtables as well as the preliminary staff report, one such commenter noted the legitimate interest consumers have in controlling how companies collect and use aggregated or de-identified data, browser fingerprints,[92] and other types of non-PII.[93] Another company questioned the notion of distinguishing between PII and non-PII as a way to determine what data to protect.[94] Supporting a scaled approach rather than a bright line distinction, this commenter noted that all data derived from individuals deserves some level of protection.[95]

Other commenters representing industry opposed the proposed framework's application to non-PII that can be reasonably linked to a consumer, computer, or device.[96] These commenters asserted that the risks associated with the collection and use of data that does not contain PII are simply not the same as the risks associated with PII. They also claimed a lack of evidence demonstrating that consumers have the same privacy interest in non-PII as they do with the collection and use of PII. Instead of applying the framework to non-PII, these commenters recommended the Commission support efforts to de-identify data.

Overall, the comments reflect a general acknowledgment that the traditional distinction between PII and non-PII has blurred and that it is appropriate to more comprehensively examine data to determine the data's privacy implications.[97] However, some commenters, including some of those cited above, argued that the proposed framework's "linkability" standard is potentially too open-ended to be practical.[98] One industry organization asserted, for instance, that if given enough time and resources, any data may be linkable to an

---

90   *Comment of Electronic Frontier Foundation*, cmt. #00400, at 4 (citing Julia Angwin & Steve Stecklow, *'Scrapers' Dig Deep for Data on Web*, WALL ST. J., Oct. 12, 2010, *available at* http://online.wsj.com/article/SB10001424052748703358504575544381288117888.html); *Sorrell v. IMS Health Inc.*, 131 S. Ct. 2653 (2011).

91   *Comment of Mozilla*, cmt. #00480, at 4-5; *Comment of Google Inc.*, cmt. #00417, at 8.

92   The term "browser fingerprints" refers to the specific combination of characteristics – such as system fonts, software, and installed plugins – that are typically made available by a consumer's browser to any website visited. These characteristics can be used to uniquely identify computers, cell phones, or other devices. Browser fingerprinting does not rely on cookies. *See* Erik Larkin, *Browser Fingerprinting Can ID You Without Cookies*, PCWORLD, Jan. 29, 2010, *available at* http://www.pcworld.com/article/188161/browser_fingerprinting_can_id_you_without_cookies.html.

93   *Comment of Mozilla*, cmt. #00480, at 4-5 (citing FTC, *Protecting Consumer Privacy in an Era of Rapid Change: A Proposed Framework for Businesses and Policymakers*, Preliminary FTC Staff Report, at 36-37 (Dec. 2010), *available at* http://www.ftc.gov/os/2010/12/101201privacyreport.pdf).

94   *Comment of Google Inc.*, cmt. #00417, at 8.

95   *Comment of Google Inc.*, cmt. #00417, at 8.

96   *Comment of Direct Marketing Ass'n, Inc.*, cmt. #00449, at 13-14; *Comment of National Cable & Telecommunications Ass'n*, cmt. #00432, at 13-17.

97   *See Comment of AT&T Inc.*, cmt. #00420, at 13-15; *Comment of Center for Democracy & Technology* (Feb. 18, 2011), cmt. #00469, at 3-4; *Comment of CTIA - The Wireless Ass'n*, cmt. #00375, at 3-4; *Comment of Consumers Union*, cmt. #00362, at 4-5; *Comment of Electronic Frontier Foundation*, cmt. #00400, at 1-4; *Comment of Google Inc.*, cmt. #00417, at 7-8; *Comment of Mozilla*, cmt. #00480, at 4-6; *Comment of Phorm Inc.*, cmt. #00353, at 3-4.

98   *Comment of AT&T Inc.*, cmt. #00420, at 13; Comment of *CTIA - The Wireless Ass'n*, cmt. #00375 at 3-4; *Comment of Google Inc.*, cmt. #00417, at 8; *Comment of Phorm Inc.*, cmt. #00353, at 4.

individual.[99] In addition, commenters stated that requiring the same level of protection for all data would undermine companies' incentive to avoid collecting data that is more easily identified or to take steps to de-identify the data they collect and use.[100] Other commenters argued that applying the framework to data that is potentially linkable could conflict with the framework's privacy by design concept, as companies could be forced to collect more information about consumers than they otherwise would in order to be able to provide those consumers with effective notice, choice, or access.[101] To address these concerns, some commenters proposed limiting the framework to data that is actually linked to a specific consumer, computer, or device.[102]

One commenter recommended that the Commission clarify that the reasonably linkable standard means non-public data that can be linked with *reasonable effort*.[103] This commenter also stated that the framework should exclude data that, through contract or by virtue of internal controls, will not be linked with a particular consumer. Taking a similar approach, another commenter suggested that the framework should apply to data that is reasonably likely to relate to an identifiable consumer.[104] This commenter also noted that a company could commit through its privacy policy that it would only maintain or use data in a de-identified form and that such a commitment would be enforceable under Section 5 of the FTC Act.[105]

The Commission believes there is sufficient support from commenters representing an array of perspectives – including consumer and privacy advocates as well as of industry representatives – for the framework's application to data that, while not yet linked to a particular consumer, computer, or device, may reasonably become so. There is significant evidence demonstrating that technological advances and the ability to combine disparate pieces of data can lead to identification of a consumer, computer, or device even if the individual pieces of data do not constitute PII.[106] Moreover, not only is it possible to re-identify non-PII data through various means,[107] businesses have strong incentives to actually do so.

In response to the comments, to provide greater certainty for companies that collect and use consumer data, the Commission provides additional clarification on the application of the reasonable linkability standard to describe how companies can take appropriate steps to minimize such linkability. Under the final

---

99   *Comment of GS1*, cmt. #00439, at 2.

100 *Comment of AT&T Inc.*, cmt. #00420, at 13-14; *Comment of CTIA - The Wireless Ass'n*, cmt. #00375, at 4; *Comment of Experian*, cmt. #00398, at 11; *Comment of National Cable & Telecommunications Ass'n*, cmt. #00432, at 16.

101 *Comment of United States Council for International Business*, cmt. #00366, at 1; *Comment of Phorm Inc.*, cmt. #00353, at 3.

102 *Comment of Retail Industry Leaders Ass'n*, cmt. #00352, at 4; *Comment of Yahoo! Inc.*, cmt. #00444, at 3-4; *Comment of GS1*, cmt. #00439, at 3.

103 *Comment of AT&T Inc.*, cmt. #00420, at 13.

104 *Comment of Intel Corp.*, cmt. #00246, at 9.

105 *Comment of Intel Corp.*, cmt. #00246, at 9.

106 FTC, *Protecting Consumer Privacy in an Era of Rapid Change: A Proposed Framework for Businesses and Policymakers, Preliminary FTC Staff Report*, 35-38 (Dec. 2010), *available at* http://www.ftc.gov/os/2010/12/101201privacyreport.pdf; *Comment of Center for Democracy & Technology*, cmt. #00469, at 3; *Comment of Statz, Inc.*, cmt. #00377, at 11-12. *See supra* note 89.

107 *See* FTC, *FTC Staff Report: Self-Regulatory Principles for Online Behavioral Advertising*, 21-24, 43-45 (Feb. 2009), *available at* http://www.ftc.gov/os/2009/02/P0085400behavadreport.pdf; Paul M. Schwartz & Daniel J. Solove, *The PII Problem: Privacy and a New Concept of Personally Identifiable Information*, 86 N.Y.U. L. Rev. 1814, 1836-1848 (2011).

framework, a company's data would not be reasonably linkable to a particular consumer or device to the extent that the company implements three significant protections for that data.

First, the company must take reasonable measures to ensure that the data is de-identified. This means that the company must achieve a reasonable level of justified confidence that the data cannot reasonably be used to infer information about, or otherwise be linked to, a particular consumer, computer, or other device. Consistent with the Commission's approach in its data security cases,[108] what qualifies as a reasonable level of justified confidence depends upon the particular circumstances, including the available methods and technologies. In addition, the nature of the data at issue and the purposes for which it will be used are also relevant. Thus, for example, whether a company publishes data externally affects whether the steps it has taken to de-identify data are considered reasonable. The standard is not an absolute one; rather, companies must take reasonable steps to ensure that data is de-identified.

Depending on the circumstances, a variety of technical approaches to de-identification may be reasonable, such as deletion or modification of data fields, the addition of sufficient "noise" to data, statistical sampling, or the use of aggregate or synthetic data.[109] The Commission encourages companies and researchers to continue innovating in the development and evaluation of new and better approaches to de-identification. FTC staff will continue to monitor and assess the state of the art in de-identification.

Second, a company must publicly commit to maintain and use the data in a de-identified fashion, and not to attempt to re-identify the data. Thus, if a company does take steps to re-identify such data, its conduct could be actionable under Section 5 of the FTC Act.

Third, if a company makes such de-identified data available to other companies – whether service providers or other third parties – it should contractually prohibit such entities from attempting to re-identify the data. The company that transfers or otherwise makes the data available should exercise reasonable oversight to monitor compliance with these contractual provisions and take appropriate steps to address contractual violations.[110]

FTC staff's letter closing its investigation of Netflix, arising from the company's plan to release purportedly anonymous consumer data to improve its movie recommendation algorithm, provides a good illustration of these concepts. In response to the privacy concerns that FTC staff and others raised, Netflix revised its initial plan to publicly release the data. The company agreed to narrow any such release of data to certain researchers. The letter details Netflix's commitment to implement a number of "operational

---

108 The Commission's approach in data security cases is a flexible one. Where a company has offered assurances to consumers that it has implemented reasonable security measures, the Commission assesses the reasonableness based, among other things, on the sensitivity of the information collected, the measures the company has implemented to protect such information, and whether the company has taken action to address and prevent well-known and easily addressable security vulnerabilities.

109 See, e.g., Cynthia Dwork, A Firm Foundation for Private Data Analysis, 54 COMM. OF THE ACM 86-95 (2011), available at http://research.microsoft.com/pubs/116123/dwork_cacm.pdf, and references cited therein.

110 See In the Matter of Superior Mortg. Corp., FTC Docket No. C-4153 (Dec. 14, 2005), available at, http://www.ftc.gov/os/caselist/0523136/0523136.shtm (alleging a violation of the GLB Safeguards Rule for, among other things, a failure to ensure that service providers were providing appropriate security for customer information and addressing known security risks in a timely manner).

safeguards to prevent the data from being used to re-identify consumers."[111] If it chose to share such data with third parties, Netflix stated that it would limit access "only to researchers who contractually agree to specific limitations on its use."[112]

Accordingly, as long as (1) a given data set is not reasonably identifiable, (2) the company publicly commits not to re-identify it, and (3) the company requires any downstream users of the data to keep it in de-identified form, that data will fall outside the scope of the framework.[113]

This clarification of the framework's reasonable linkability standard is designed to help address the concern that the standard is overly broad. Further, the clarification gives companies an incentive to collect and use data in a form that makes it less likely the data will be linked to a particular consumer or device, thereby promoting privacy. Additionally, by calling for companies to publicly commit to the steps they take, the framework promotes accountability.[114]

Consistent with the discussion above, the Commission restates the framework's scope as follows.

Final Scope: The framework applies to all commercial entities that collect or use consumer data that can be reasonably linked to a specific consumer, computer, or other device, unless the entity collects only non-sensitive data from fewer than 5,000 consumers per year and does not share the data with third parties.

B. PRIVACY BY DESIGN

Baseline Principle: Companies should promote consumer privacy throughout their organizations and at every stage of the development of their products and services.

The preliminary staff report called on companies to promote consumer privacy throughout their organizations and at every stage of the development of their products and services. Although many companies already incorporate substantive and procedural privacy protections into their business practices, industry should implement privacy by design more systematically. A number of commenters, including those representing industry, supported staff's call that companies "build in" privacy, with several of these commenters citing to the broad international recognition and adoption of privacy by design.[115] The Commission is encouraged to see broad support for this concept, particularly in light of the increasingly global nature of data transfers.

---

111 Letter from Maneesha Mithal, Assoc. Dir., Div. of Privacy & Identity Prot., FTC, to Reed Freeman, Morrison & Foerster LLP, Counsel for Netflix, 2 (Mar. 12, 2010), *available at* http://www.ftc.gov/os/closings/100312netflixletter.pdf (closing letter).

112 *Id.*

113 To the extent that a company maintains and uses both data that is identifiable and data that it has taken steps to de-identify as outlined here, the company should silo the data separately.

114 A company that violates its policy against re-identifying data could be subject to liability under the FTC Act or other laws.

115 *Comment of Office of the Information and Privacy Commissioner of Ontario*, cmt. #00239, at 2-3; *Comment of Intel Corp.*, cmt. #00246, at 12-13; *Comment of CNIL*, cmt. #00298, at 2-3.

In calling for privacy by design, staff advocated for the implementation of substantive privacy protections – such as data security, limitations on data collection and retention, and data accuracy – as well as procedural safeguards aimed at integrating the substantive principles into a company's everyday business operations. By shifting burdens away from consumers and placing obligations on businesses to treat consumer data in a responsible manner, these principles should afford consumers basic privacy protections without forcing them to read long, incomprehensible privacy notices to learn and make choices about a company's privacy practices. Although the Commission has not changed the proposed "privacy by design" principles, it responds to a number of comments, as discussed below.

1. THE SUBSTANTIVE PRINCIPLES: DATA SECURITY, REASONABLE COLLECTION LIMITS, SOUND RETENTION PRACTICES, AND DATA ACCURACY.

Proposed Principle: Companies should incorporate substantive privacy protections into their practices, such as data security, reasonable collection limits, sound retention practices, and data accuracy.

a. Should Additional Substantive Principles Be Identified?

Responding to a question about whether the final framework should identify additional substantive protections, several commenters suggested incorporating the additional principles articulated in the 1980 OECD Privacy Guidelines.[116] One commenter also proposed adding the "right to be forgotten," which would allow consumers to withdraw data posted online about themselves at any point.[117] This concept has gained importance as people post more information about themselves online without fully appreciating the implications of such data sharing or the persistence of online data over time.[118] In supporting an expansive view of privacy by design, a consumer advocacy group noted that the individual elements and principles of the proposed framework should work together holistically.[119]

In response, the Commission notes that the framework already embodies all the concepts in the 1980 OECD privacy guidelines, although with some updates and changes in emphasis. For example, privacy by design includes the collection limitation, data quality, and security principles. Additionally, the framework's simplified choice and transparency components, discussed below, encompass the OECD principles of purpose specification, use limitation, individual participation, and openness. The framework also adopts the

---

116 *Comment of CNIL*, cmt. #00298, at 2; *Comment of the Information Commissioner's Office of the UK*, cmt. #00249, at 2; *Comment of World Privacy Forum*, cmt. #00369, at 7; *Comment of Intel Corp.*, cmt. #00246, at 4; *see also* Organisation for Economic Co-operation & Development, *OECD Guidelines on the Protection of Privacy and Transborder Flows of Personal Data* (Sept. 1980), *available at* http://www.oecd.org/document/18/0,3343,en_2649_34255_1815186_1_1_1_1,00&&en-USS_01DBC.html (these principles include purpose specification, individual participation, accountability, and principles to govern cross-border data transfers). Another commenter called for baseline legislation based on the Fair Information Practice Principles and the principles outlined in the 1974 Privacy Act. *Comment of Electronic Privacy Information Center*, cmt. #00386, at 17-20.

117 *Comment of CNIL*, cmt. #00298, at 3.

118 The concept of the "right to be forgotten," and its importance to young consumers, is discussed in more detail below in the Transparency Section, *infra* at Section IV.D.2.b.

119 *Comment of Consumers Union*, cmt. #00362, at 1-2, 5-9, 18-19.

OECD principle that companies must be accountable for their privacy practices. Specifically, the framework calls on companies to implement procedures – such as designating a person responsible for privacy, training employees, and ensuring adequate oversight of third parties – to help ensure that they are implementing appropriate substantive privacy protections. The framework also calls on industry to increase efforts to educate consumers about the commercial collection and use of their data and the available privacy tools. In addition, there are aspects of the proposed "right to be forgotten" in the final framework, which calls on companies to (1) delete consumer data that they no longer need and (2) allow consumers to access their data and in appropriate cases suppress or delete it.[120]

All of the principles articulated in the preliminary staff report are intended to work together to shift the burden for protecting privacy away from consumers and to encourage companies to make strong privacy protections the default. Reasonable collection limits and data disposal policies work in tandem with streamlined notices and improved consumer choice mechanisms. Together, they function to provide substantive protections by placing reasonable limits on the collection, use, and retention of consumer data to more closely align with consumer expectations, while also raising consumer awareness about the nature and extent of data collection, use, and third-party sharing, and the choices available to them.

b. Data Security: Companies Must Provide Reasonable Security for Consumer Data.

It is well settled that companies must provide reasonable security for consumer data. The Commission has a long history of enforcing data security obligations under Section 5 of the FTC Act, the FCRA and the GLBA. Since 2001, the FTC has brought 36 cases under these laws, charging that businesses failed to appropriately protect consumers' personal information. Since issuance of the preliminary staff report alone, the Commission has resolved seven data security actions against resellers of sensitive consumer report information, service providers that process employee data, a college savings program, and a social media service.[121] In addition to the federal laws the FTC enforces, companies are subject to a variety of

---

120 *See In the Matter of Facebook, Inc.*, FTC File No. 092 3184 (Nov. 29, 2011) (proposed consent order), *available at* http://www.ftc.gov/os/caselist/0923184/index.shtm (requiring Facebook to make inaccessible within thirty days data that a user deletes); *see also* Do Not Track Kids Act of 2011, H.R. 1895, 112th Cong. (2011).

121 *In the Matter of Upromise, Inc.*, FTC File No. 102 3116 (Jan. 18, 2012) (proposed consent order), *available at* http://www.ftc.gov/os/caselist/1023116/index.shtm; *In the Matter of ACRAnet, Inc.*, FTC Docket No. C-4331(Aug. 17, 2011) (consent order), *available at* http://ftc.gov/os/caselist/0923088/index.shtm; *In the Matter of Fajilan & Assocs., Inc.*, FTC Docket No. C-4332 (Aug. 17, 2011) (consent order), *available at* http://ftc.gov/os/caselist/0923089/index.shtm; *In the Matter of SettlementOne Credit Corp.*, FTC Docket No. C-4330 (Aug. 17, 2011) (consent order), *available at* http://ftc.gov/os/caselist/0823208/index.shtm; *In the Matter of Lookout Servs., Inc.*, FTC Docket No. C-4326 (June 15, 2011) (consent order), *available at* http://www.ftc.gov/os/caselist/102376/index.shtm; *In the Matter of Ceridian Corp.*, FTC Docket No. C-4325 (June 8, 2011) (consent order), *available at* http://www.ftc.gov/os/caselist/1023160/index.shtm; *In the Matter of Twitter, Inc.*, FTC Docket No. C-4316 (Mar. 11, 2011) (consent order), *available at* http://www.ftc.gov/os/caselist/0923093/index.shtm.

other federal and state law obligations. In some industries, such as banking, federal regulators have given additional guidance on how to define reasonable security.[122]

The Commission also promotes better data security through consumer and business education. For example, the FTC sponsors OnGuard Online, a website to educate consumers about basic computer security.[123] Since the Commission issued the preliminary staff report there have been over 1.5 million unique visits to OnGuard Online and its Spanish-language counterpart Alerta en Línea. The Commission's business outreach includes general advice about data security as well as specific advice about emerging topics.[124]

The Commission also notes that the private sector has implemented a variety of initiatives in the security area, including the Payment Card Institute Data Security Standards for payment card data, the SANS Institute's security policy templates, and standards and best practices guidelines for the financial services industry provided by BITS, the technology policy division of the Financial Services Roundtable.[125] These standards can provide useful guidance on appropriate data security measures that organizations should implement for specific types of consumer data or in specific industries. The Commission further calls on industry to develop and implement best data security practices for additional industry sectors and other types of consumer data.

Because this issue is important to consumers and because businesses have existing legal and self-regulatory obligations, many individual companies have placed great emphasis and resources on maintaining reasonable security. For example, Google has cited certain security features in its products, including default SSL encryption for Gmail and security features in its Chrome browser.[126] Similarly, Mozilla has noted that

---

122 *See, e.g.*, Federal Financial Institutions Examination Council ("FFIEC"), *Information Society IT Examination Handbook* (July 2006), *available at* http://ithandbook.ffiec.gov/it-booklets/information-security.aspx; Letter from Richard Spillenkothen, Dir., Div. of Banking Supervision & Regulation, Bd. of Governors of the Fed. Reserve Sys., *SRO1-11: Identity Theft and Pretext Calling* (Apr. 26, 2011), *available at* http://www.federalreserve.gov/boarddocs/srletters/2001/sr0111.htm (guidance on pretexting and identity theft); Securities & Exchange Commission, *CF Disclosure Guidance: Topic No. 2, on Cybersecurity* (Oct. 13, 2011), *available at* http://www.sec.gov/divisions/corpfin/guidance/cfguidance-topic2.htm; U.S. Small Business Administration, Information Security Guidance, http://www.sba.gov/content/information-security; National Institute of Standards & Technology, Computer Security Division, *Computer Security Resource Center*, *available at* http://csrc.nist.gov/groups/SMA/sbc/index.html; HHS, Health Information Privacy, *available at* http://www.hhs.gov/ocr/privacy/hipaa/understanding/coveredentities/index.html (guidance and educational materials for entities required to comply with the HIPPA Privacy and Security Rules); Centers from Medicare and Medicaid Services, *Educational Materials*, *available at* http://www.cms.gov/EducationMaterials/ (educational materials for HIPPA compliance).

123 FTC, OnGuard Online, http://onguardonline.gov/.

124 *See* FTC, *Protecting Personal Information: A Guide for Business* (Nov. 2011), *available at* http://business.ftc.gov/documents/bus69-protecting-personal-information-guide-business; *see generally* FTC, Bureau of Consumer Protection Business Center, Data Security Guidance, *available at* http://business.ftc.gov/privacy-and-security/data-security.

125 *See* PCI Security Standards Council, *PCI SSC Data Security Standards Overview*, *available at* https://www.pcisecuritystandards.org/security_standards/; SANS Institute, *Information Security Policy Templates*, *available at* http://www.sans.org/security-resources/policies/; BITS, *Financial Services Roundtable BITS Publications*, *available at* http://www.bits.org/publications/index.php; *see also, e.g.*, Better Business Bureau, *Security and Privacy – Made Simpler: Manageable Guidelines to help You Protect Your Customers' Security & Privacy from Identity Theft & Fraud*, *available at* http://www.bbb.org/us/storage/16/documents/SecurityPrivacyMadeSimpler.pdf; National Cyber Security Alliance, *For Business*, http://www.staysafeonline.org/for-business (guidance for small and midsize businesses); Direct Marketing Association, *Information Security: Safeguarding Personal Data in Your Care* (May 2005), *available at* http://www.the-dma.org/privacy/InfoSecData.pdf; Messaging Anti-Abuse Working Group & Anti-Phishing Working Group, *Anti-Phishing Best Practices for ISPs and Mailbox Providers* (July 2006), *available at* http://www.antiphishing.org/reports/bestpracticesforisps.pdf.

126 *Comment of Google Inc.*, cmt. #00417, at 2-3.

its cloud storage system encrypts user data using SSL communication.[127] Likewise, Twitter has implemented encryption by default for users logged into its system.[128] The Commission commends these efforts and calls on companies to continue to look for additional ways to build data security into products and services from the design stage.

Finally, the Commission reiterates its call for Congress to enact data security and breach notification legislation. To help deter violations, such legislation should authorize the Commission to seek civil penalties.

c. Reasonable Collection Limitation: Companies Should Limit Their Collection of Data.

The preliminary staff report called on companies to collect only the data they need to accomplish a specific business purpose. Many commenters expressed support for the general principle that companies should limit the information they collect from consumers.[129] Despite the broad support for the concept, however, many companies argued for a flexible approach based on concerns that allowing companies to collect data only for existing business needs would harm innovation and deny consumers new products and services.[130] One commenter cited Netflix's video recommendation feature as an example of how secondary uses of data can create consumer benefits. The commenter noted that Netflix originally collected information about subscribers' movie preferences in order to send the specific videos requested, but later used this information as the foundation for generating personalized recommendations to its subscribers.[131]

In addition, commenters raised concerns about who decides what a "specific business purpose" is.[132] For example, one purpose for collecting data is to sell it to third parties in order to monetize a service and provide it to consumers for free. Would collecting data for this purpose be a specific business purpose? If not, is the only alternative to charge consumers for the service, and would this result be better for consumers?

As an alternative to limiting collection to accomplish a "specific business purpose," many commenters advocated limiting collection to business purposes *that are clearly articulated*. This is akin to the Fair Information Practice Principle of "purpose specification," which holds that companies should specify to consumers all of the purposes for which information is collected at the time of collection. One commenter supported purpose specification statements in general categories to allow innovation and avoid making privacy policies overly complex.[133]

---

127 *Comment of Mozilla*, cmt. #00480, at 7.

128 *See* Chloe Albanesius, *Twitter Adds Always-On Encryption*, PC Magazine, Feb. 12, 2012, http://www.pcmag.com/article2/0,2817,2400252,00.asp.

129 *See, e.g., Comment of Intel Corp.*, cmt. #00246, at 4-5, 7, 40-41; *Comment of Electronic Frontier Foundation*, cmt. #00400, at 4-6; *Comment of Center for Democracy & Technology*, cmt. #00469, at 4-5; *Comment of Electronic Privacy Information Center*, cmt. #00386, at 18.

130 *See, e.g., Comment of Facebook, Inc.*, cmt. #00413, at 2, 7-8, 18; *Comment of Google Inc.*, cmt. #00417, at 4; *Comment of Direct Marketing Ass'n, Inc.*, cmt. #00449, at 14-15; *Comment of Intuit, Inc.*, cmt. #00348, at 5, 9; *Comment of TRUSTe*, cmt. #00450, at 9.

131 *Comment of Facebook, Inc.*, cmt. #00413, at 7-8.

132 *See Comment of SAS*, cmt. #00415, at 51; *Comment of Yahoo! Inc.*, cmt. #00444, at 5.

133 *Comment of Yahoo! Inc.*, cmt. #00444, at 5.

The Commission recognizes the need for flexibility to permit innovative new uses of data that benefit consumers. At the same time, in order to protect consumer privacy, there must be some reasonable limit on the collection of consumer data. General statements in privacy policies, however, are not an appropriate tool to ensure such a limit because companies have an incentive to make vague promises that would permit them to do virtually anything with consumer data.

Accordingly, the Commission clarifies the collection limitation principle of the framework as follows: Companies should limit data collection to that which is consistent with the context of a particular transaction or the consumer's relationship with the business, or as required or specifically authorized by law.[134] For any data collection that is inconsistent with these contexts, companies should make appropriate disclosures to consumers at a relevant time and in a prominent manner – outside of a privacy policy or other legal document. This clarification of the collection limitation principle is intended to help companies assess whether their data collection is consistent with what a consumer might expect; if it is not, they should provide prominent notice and choice. (For a further discussion of this point, see *infra* Section IV.C.2.) This approach is consistent with the Administration's Consumer Privacy Bill of Rights, which includes a Respect for Context principle that limits the use of consumer data to those purposes consistent with the context in which consumers originally disclosed the data.[135]

One example of a company innovating around the concept of privacy by design through collection limitation is the Graduate Management Admission Council ("GMAC"). This entity previously collected fingerprints from individuals taking the Graduate Management Admission Test. After concerns were raised about individuals' fingerprints being cross-referenced against criminal databases, GMAC developed a system that allowed for collection of palm prints that could be used solely for test-taking purposes.[136] The palm print technology is as accurate as fingerprinting but less susceptible to "function creep" over time than the taking of fingerprints, because palm prints are not widely used as a common identifier. GMAC received a privacy innovation award for small businesses for its work in this area.

d. Sound Data Retention: Companies Should Implement Reasonable Data Retention and Disposal Policies.

Similar to the concerns raised about collection limits, many commenters expressed concern about limiting retention of consumer data, asserting that such limits would harm innovation. Trade associations and businesses requested a flexible standard for data retention to allow companies to develop new products

---

134 This approach mirrors the revised standard for determining whether a particular data practice warrants consumer choice (see *infra* at section IV.C.1.a.) and is consistent with a number of commenters' calls for considering the context in which a particular practice takes place. *See, e.g., Comment of CTIA - The Wireless Ass'n*, cmt. #00375, at 2-4; *Comment of Consumer Data Industry Ass'n*, cmt. #00363, at 5; *Comment of TRUSTe*, cmt. #00450, at 3.

135 *See* White House, *Consumer Data Privacy in a Networked World: A Framework for Protecting Privacy and Promoting Innovation in the Global Digital Economy*, 15-19, (Feb. 2012), *available at* http://www.whitehouse.gov/sites/default/files/privacy-final.pdf. For a further discussion of this point, see *infra* at Section IV.C.1.a.

136 *See* Jay Cline, *GMAC: Navigating EU Approval for Advanced Biomterics*, INSIDE PRIVACY BLOG (Oct. 15, 2010), https://www. privacyassociation.org/publications/2010_10_20_gmac_navigating_eu_approval_for_advanced_biometrics (explaining GMAC's adoption of palm print technology); *cf.* Kashmir Hill, *Why 'Privacy by Design' is the New Corporate Hotness*, FORBES, July 28, 2011, *available at* http://www.forbes.com/sites/kashmirhill/2011/07/28/why-privacy-by-design-is-the-new-corporate-hotness/.

and other uses of data that provide benefits to consumers.[137] One company raised concerns about prescriptive retention periods, arguing that retention standards instead should be based on business need, the type and location of data at issue, operational issues, and legal requirements.[138] Other commenters noted that retention limits should be sufficiently flexible to accommodate requests from law enforcement or other legitimate business purposes, such as the need of a mortgage banker to retain information about a consumer's payment history.[139] Some commenters suggested that the Commission's focus should be on data security and proper handling of consumer data, rather than on retention limits.[140]

In contrast, some consumer groups advocated specific retention periods. For example, one such commenter cited a proposal made by a consortium of consumer groups in 2009 that companies that collect data for online behavioral advertising should limit their retention of the data to three months and that companies that retained their online behavioral advertising data for only 24 hours may not need to obtain consumer consent for their data collection and use.[141] Others stated that it might be appropriate for the FTC to recommend industry-specific retention periods after a public consultation.[142]

The Commission confirms its conclusion that companies should implement reasonable restrictions on the retention of data and should dispose of it once the data has outlived the legitimate purpose for which it was collected.[143] Retention periods, however, can be flexible and scaled according to the type of relationship and use of the data; for example, there may be legitimate reasons for certain companies that have a direct relationship with customers to retain some data for an extended period of time. A mortgage company will maintain data for the life of the mortgage to ensure accurate payment tracking; an auto dealer will retain data from its customers for years to manage service records and inform its customers of new offers. These long retention periods help maintain productive customer relationships. This analysis does not, however, apply to all data collection scenarios. A number of commenters noted that online behavioral advertising data often becomes stale quickly and need not be retained long.[144] For example, a consumer researching hotels in a particular city for an upcoming vacation is unlikely to be interested in continuing to see hotel advertisements after the trip is completed. Indefinite retention of data about the consumer's interest in finding a hotel for a particular weekend serves little purpose and could result in marketers sending the consumer irrelevant advertising.

---

137 *See Comment of CTIA - The Wireless Ass'n*, cmt. #00375, at 2-4, 14; *Comment of American Catalog Mailers Ass'n*, cmt. #000424, at 5; *Comment of IBM*, cmt. #00433, at 4; *Comment of Intuit, Inc.*, cmt. #00348, at 9.

138 *Comment of Verizon*, cmt. #00428, at 10-11.

139 *See, e.g., Comment of CTIA - The Wireless Ass'n*, cmt. #00375, at 14.

140 *Comment of Yahoo! Inc.*, cmt. #00444, at 6; *see also Comment of American Catalog Mailers Ass'n*, cmt. #00424, at 3-4.

141 *Comment of Consumer Federation of America*, cmt. #00358, at 4 (citing *Legislative Primer: Online Behavioral Tracking and Targeting Concerns and Solutions from the Perspective of the Center for Digital Democracy and U.S. PIRG, Consumer Federation of America, Consumers Union, Consumer Watchdog, Electronic Frontier Foundation, Privacy Lives, Privacy Rights Clearinghouse, Privacy Times, U.S. Public Interest Research group, The World Privacy Forum* (Sept. 2009), *available at* http://www.consumerfed. org/elements/www.consumerfed.org/file/OnlinePrivacyLegPrimerSEPT09.pdf).

142 *Comment of Center for Democracy & Technology*, cmt. #00469, at 6 ("Flexible approaches to data retention should not, however, give *carte blanche* to companies to maintain consumer data after it has outlived its reasonable usefulness.").

143 In the alternative, companies may consider taking steps to de-identify the data they maintain, as discussed above.

144 *See Comment of Consumers Union*, cmt. #00362, at 8.

In determining when to dispose of data, as well as limitations on collection described above, companies should also take into account the nature of the data they collect. For example, consider a company that develops an online interactive game as part of a marketing campaign directed to teens. The company should first assess whether it needs to collect the teens' data as part of the game, and if so, how it could limit the data collected, such as by allowing teens to create their own username instead of using a real name and email address. If the company decides to collect the data, it should consider disposing of it even more quickly than it would if it collected adults' data. Similarly, recognizing the sensitivity of data such as a particular consumer's real time location, companies should take special care to delete this data as soon as possible, consistent with the services they provide to consumers.

Although restrictions may be tailored to the nature of the company's business and the data at issue, companies should develop clear standards and train its employees to follow them. Trade associations and self-regulatory groups also should be more proactive in providing guidance to their members about retention and data destruction policies. Accordingly, the Commission calls on industry groups from all sectors – the online advertising industry, online publishers, mobile participants, social networks, data brokers and others – to do more to provide guidance in this area. Similarly, the Commission generally supports the exploration of efforts to develop additional mechanisms, such as the "eraser button" for social media discussed below,[145] to allow consumers to manage and, where appropriate, require companies to delete the information consumers have submitted.

e. Accuracy: Companies should maintain reasonable accuracy of consumers' data.

The preliminary staff report called on companies to take reasonable steps to ensure the accuracy of the data they collect and maintain, particularly if such data could cause significant harm or be used to deny consumers services. Similar to concerns raised about collection limits and retention periods, commenters opposed rigid accuracy standards,[146] and noted that the FCRA already imposes accuracy standards in certain contexts.[147] One commenter highlighted the challenges of providing the same levels of accuracy for non-identifiable data versus data that is identifiable.[148]

To address these challenges, some commenters stated that a sliding scale approach should be followed, particularly for marketing data. These commenters stated that marketing data is not used for eligibility purposes and that, if inaccurate, the only harm a consumer may experience is an irrelevant advertisement.[149] Providing enhanced accuracy standards for marketing data would raise additional privacy and data security concerns,[150] as additional information may need to be added to marketing databases to increase accuracy.[151]

---

145 See *infra* at Section IV.D.2.b.

146 *See Comment of Experian*, cmt. #00398, at 2.

147 *See Comment of SIFMA*, cmt. #00265, at 4.

148 *Comment of Phorm Inc.*, cmt. #00353, at 4.

149 *Comment of Experian*, cmt. #00398, at 11 (arguing against enhanced standards for accuracy, access, and correction for marketing data); *see also Comment of Yahoo! Inc.*, cmt. #00444, at 6-7.

150 *Id.*

151 *Cf. Comment of Yahoo! Inc.*, cmt. #00444, at 7 (arguing that it would be costly, time consuming, and contrary to privacy objectives to verify the accuracy of user registration information such as gender, age or hometown).

The Commission agrees that the best approach to improving the accuracy of the consumer data companies collect and maintain is a flexible one, scaled to the intended use and sensitivity of the information. Thus, for example, companies using data for marketing purposes need not take special measures to ensure the accuracy of the information they maintain. Companies using data to make decisions about consumers' eligibility for benefits should take much more robust measures to ensure accuracy, including allowing consumers access to the data and the opportunity to correct erroneous information.[152]

Final Principle: Companies should incorporate substantive privacy protections into their practices, such as data security, reasonable collection limits, sound retention and disposal practices, and data accuracy.

2. COMPANIES SHOULD ADOPT PROCEDURAL PROTECTIONS TO IMPLEMENT THE SUBSTANTIVE PRINCIPLES.

Proposed Principle: Companies should maintain comprehensive data management procedures throughout the life cycle of their products and services.

In addition to the substantive principles articulated above, the preliminary staff report called for organizations to maintain comprehensive data management procedures, such as designating personnel responsible for employee privacy training and regularly assessing the privacy impact of specific practices, products, and services. Many commenters supported this call for accountability within an organization.[153] Commenters noted that privacy risk assessments promote accountability, and help identify and address privacy issues.[154] One commenter stated that privacy risk assessments should be an ongoing process, and findings should be used to update internal procedures.[155] The Commission agrees that companies should implement accountability mechanisms and conduct regular privacy risk assessments to ensure that privacy issues are addressed throughout an organization.

The preliminary staff report also called on companies to "consider privacy issues systemically, at all stages of the design and development of their products and services." A range of commenters supported the principle of "baking" privacy into the product development process.[156] One commenter stated that this approach of including privacy considerations in the product development process was preferable to requiring

---

152 See *infra* at Section IV.D.2. The Commission notes that some privacy-enhancing technologies operate by introducing deliberate "noise" into data. The data accuracy principle is not intended to rule out the appropriate use of these methods, provided that the entity using them notifies any recipients of the data that it is inaccurate.

153 *See, e.g., Comment of The Centre for Information Policy Leadership at Hunton & Williams LLP*, cmt. #00360, at 2-3; *Comment of Intel Corp.*, cmt. #00246, at 6; *Comment of Office of the Information & Privacy Commissioner of Ontario*, cmt. #00239, at 3.

154 *Comment of GS1*, cmt. #00439, at 3; *Comment of Office of the Information & Privacy Commissioner of Ontario*, cmt. #00239, at 6.

155 *Comment of Office of the Information & Privacy Commissioner of Ontario*, cmt. #00239, at 7.

156 *Comment of Intel Corp.*, cmt. #00246, at 6; *Comment of United States Council for International Business*, cmt. #00366, at 2; *Comment of Consumer Federation of America*, cmt. #00358, at 3.

after-the-fact reviews.[157] Another argued that privacy concerns should be considered from the outset, but observed that such concerns should continue to be evaluated as the product, service, or feature evolves.[158]

The Commission's recent settlements with Google and Facebook illustrate how the procedural protections discussed above might work in practice.[159] In both cases, the Commission alleged that the companies deceived consumers about the level of privacy afforded to their data.

The FTC's orders will require the companies to implement a comprehensive privacy program reasonably designed to address privacy risks related to the development and management of new and existing products and services and to protect the privacy and confidentiality of "covered information," defined broadly to mean *any* information the companies collect from or about a consumer.

The privacy programs that the orders mandate must, at a minimum, contain certain controls and procedures, including: (1) the designation of personnel responsible for the privacy program; (2) a risk assessment that, at a minimum, addresses employee training and management and product design and development; (3) the implementation of controls designed to address the risks identified; (4) appropriate oversight of service providers; and (5) evaluation and adjustment of the privacy program in light of regular testing and monitoring.[160] Companies should view the comprehensive privacy programs mandated by these consent orders as a roadmap as they implement privacy by design in their own organizations.

As an additional means of implementing the substantive privacy by design protections, the preliminary staff report advocated the use of privacy-enhancing technologies ("PETs") – such as encryption and anonymization tools – and requested comment on implementation of such technologies. One commenter stressed the need for "privacy-aware design," calling for techniques such as obfuscation and cryptography to reduce the amount of identifiable consumer data collected and used for various products and services.[161] Another stressed that PETs are a better approach in this area than rigid technical mandates.[162]

The Commission agrees that a flexible, technology-neutral approach towards developing PETs is appropriate to accommodate the rapid changes in the marketplace and will also allow companies to innovate on PETs. Accordingly, the Commission calls on companies to continue to look for new ways to protect consumer privacy throughout the life cycle of their products and services, including through the development and deployment of PETs.

Finally, Commission staff requested comment on how to apply the substantive protections articulated above to companies with legacy data systems. Many commenters supported a phase-out period for legacy data systems, giving priority to systems that contain sensitive data.[163] Another commenter suggested that

---

157 *Comment of Intel Corp.*, cmt. #00246, at 6.

158 *Comment of Zynga Inc.*, cmt. #00459, at 2.

159 Of course, the privacy programs required by these orders may not be appropriate for all types and sizes of companies that collect and use consumer data.

160 *In the Matter of Google Inc.*, FTC Docket No. C-4336 (Oct. 13, 2011) (consent order), *available at* http://www.ftc.gov/os/caselist/index.shtm.

161 *Comment of Electronic Frontier Foundation*, cmt. #00400, at 5.

162 *Comment of Business Software Alliance*, cmt. #00389, at 7-9.

163 *Comment of The Centre for Information Policy Leadership at Hunton & Williams LLP*, cmt. #00360, at 3; *Comment of the Information Commissioner's Office of the UK*, cmt. #00249, at 2; *Comment of CTIA - The Wireless Ass'n*, cmt. #00375, at 14.

imposing strict access controls on legacy data systems until they can be updated would enhance privacy.[164] Although companies need to apply the various substantive privacy by design elements to their legacy data systems, the Commission recognizes that companies need a reasonable transition period to update their systems. In applying the substantive elements to their legacy systems, companies should prioritize those systems that contain sensitive data and they should appropriately limit access to all such systems until they can update them.

> **Final Principle:** Companies should maintain comprehensive data management procedures throughout the life cycle of their products and services.

---

164 *Comment of Yahoo! Inc.*, cmt. #00444, at 7.

DATA COLLECTION AND DISPOSAL CASE STUDY: MOBILE

The rapid growth of the mobile marketplace illustrates the need for companies to implement reasonable limits on the collection, transfer, and use of consumer data and to set policies for disposing of collected data. The unique features of a mobile phone – which is highly personal, almost always on, and travels with the consumer – have facilitated unprecedented levels of data collection. Recent news reports have confirmed the extent of this ubiquitous data collection. Researchers announced, for example, that Apple had been collecting geolocation data through its mobile devices over time, and storing unencrypted data files containing this information on consumers' computers and mobile devices.[1] The Wall Street Journal has documented numerous companies gaining access to detailed information – such as age, gender, precise location, and the unique ID associated with a particular mobile device – that can then be used to track and predict consumer behavior.[2] Not surprisingly, consumers are concerned: for example, a recent Nielsen study found that a majority of smartphone app users worry about their privacy when it comes to sharing their location through a mobile device.[3] The Commission calls on companies to limit collection to data they need for a requested service or transaction. For example, a wallpaper app or an app that tracks stock quotes does not need to collect location information.[4]

The extensive collection of consumer information – particularly location information – through mobile devices also heightens the need for companies to implement reasonable policies for purging data.[5] Without data retention and disposal policies specifically tied to the stated business purpose for the data collection, location information could be used to build detailed profiles of consumer movements over time that could be used in ways not anticipated by consumers.[6] Location information is particularly useful for uniquely identifying (or re-identifying) individuals using disparate bits of data.[7] For example, a consumer can use a mobile application on her cell phone to "check in" at a restaurant for the purpose of finding and connecting with friends who are nearby. The same consumer might not expect the application provider to retain a history of restaurants she visited over time. If the application provider were to share that information with third parties, it could reveal a predictive pattern of the consumer's movements thereby exposing the consumer to a risk of harm such as stalking.[8] Taken together, the principles of reasonable collection limitation and disposal periods help to minimize the risks that information collected from or about consumers could be used in harmful or unexpected ways.

With respect to the particular concerns of location data in the mobile context, the Commission calls on entities involved in the mobile ecosystem to work together to establish standards that address data collection, transfer, use, and disposal, particularly for location data. To the extent that location data in particular is collected and shared with third parties, entities should work to provide consumers with more prominent notice and choices about such practices. Although some in the mobile ecosystem provide notice about the collection of geolocation data, not all companies have adequately disclosed the frequency or extent of the collection, transfer, and use of such data.

NOTES

1   *See* Jennifer Valentino-Devries, *Study: iPhone Keeps Tracking Data*, WALL ST. J., Apr. 21, 2011, *available at* http://online.wsj.com/article/SB10001424052748704570704576275323811369758.html.

2   *See, e.g.*, Robert Lee Hotz, *The Really Smart Phone*, WALL ST. J., Apr. 22, 2011, *available at* http://online.wsj.com/article/SB10001424052748704547604576263261679848814.html (describing how researchers are using mobile data to predict consumers' actions); Scott Thurm & Yukari Iwatane Kane, *Your Apps are Watching You*, WALL ST. J., Dec. 18, 2010, *available at* http://online.wsj.com/article/SB10001424052748704368004576027751867039730.html (documenting the data collection that occurs through many popular smartphone apps).

3   *Privacy Please! U.S. Smartphone App Users Concerned with Privacy When It Comes to Location*, NIELSENWIRE BLOG (Apr. 21, 2011), http://blog.nielsen.com/nielsenwire/online_mobile/privacy-please-u-s-smartphone-app-users-concerned-with-privacy-when-it-comes-to-location/; *see also* Ponemon Institute, *Smartphone Security: Survey of U.S. Consumers* 7 (Mar. 2011), *available at* http://aa-download.avg.com/filedir/other/Smartphone.pdf (reporting that 64% of consumers worry about their location being tracked when using their smartphones).

4   Similarly, the photo-sharing app Path faced widespread criticism for uploading its users' iPhone address books without their consent. *See, e.g.*, Mark Hachman, *Path Uploads Your Entire iPhone Contact List By Default*, PC MAGAZINE, Feb. 7, 2012, *available at* http://www.pcmag.com/article2/0,2817,2399970,00.asp.

5   The Commission is currently reviewing its COPPA Rule, including the application of COPPA to geolocation information. *See* FTC, Proposed Rule and Request for Public Comment, Children's Online Privacy Protection Rule, 76 Fed. Reg. 59,804 (Sept. 15, 2011), *available at* http://www.gpo.gov/fdsys/pkg/FR-2011-09-27/pdf/2011-24314.pdf.

6   *See* ACLU of Northern California, *Location-Based Services: Time for a Privacy Check-In*, 14-15 (Nov. 2010), *available at* http://dotrights.org/sites/default/files/lbs-white-paper.pdf.

7   *Comment of Electronic Frontier Foundation*, cmt. #00400, at 3.

8   *Cf. U.S. v. Jones*, 565 U.S. 132 S. Ct. 945, 955 (2012) (Sotomayor, J., concurring) (noting that "GPS monitoring generates a precise, comprehensive record of a person's public movements that reflects a wealth of detail about her familial, political, professional, religious, and sexual associations").

C. SIMPLIFIED CONSUMER CHOICE

Baseline Principle: Companies should simplify consumer choice.

As detailed in the preliminary staff report and in submitted comments, many consumers face challenges in understanding the nature and extent of current commercial data practices and how to exercise available choices regarding those practices. This challenge results from a number of factors including: (1) the dramatic increase in the breadth of consumer data collection and use, made possible by an ever-increasing range of technologies and business models; (2) the ability of companies, outside of certain sector-specific laws, to collect and use data without first providing consumer choice; and (3) the inadequacy of typical privacy policies as a means to effectively communicate information about the privacy choices that are offered to consumers.

To reduce the burden on those consumers who seek greater control over their data, the proposed framework called on companies that collect and use consumer data to provide easy-to-use choice mechanisms that allow consumers to control whether their data is collected and how it is used. To ensure that choice is most effective, the report stated that a company should provide the choice mechanism at a time and in a context that is relevant to consumers – generally at the point the company collects the consumer's information. At the same time, however, in recognition of the benefits of various types of data collection and use, the proposed framework identified certain "commonly accepted" categories of commercial data practices that companies can engage in without offering consumer choice.

Staff posed a variety of questions and received numerous comments regarding the proposed framework's simplified consumer choice approach. Two trade organizations argued that the framework should identify those practices for which choice is appropriate rather than making choice the general rule, subject to exceptions for certain practices.[165] The majority of commenters, however, did not challenge the proposed framework's approach of setting consumer choice as the default.[166] Instead, these commenters focused on the practicality of staff's "commonly accepted" formulation.[167] For example, several commenters questioned whether the approach was sufficiently flexible to allow for innovation.[168] Others discussed whether specific practices should fall within the categories enumerated in the preliminary staff report.[169] In addition, numerous commenters addressed the appropriate scope of the first-party marketing category and how to

---

165 *Comment of Direct Marketing Ass'n, Inc.*, cmt. #00449, at 16; *Comment of Interactive Advertising Bureau*, cmt. #00388, at 8-9.

166 Several commenters expressed support for consumer choice generally. *See, e.g., Comment of Center for Democracy & Technology*, cmt. #00469, at 11-12; *Comment of Consumer Federation of America*, cmt. #00358, at 6-12. One governmental agency, for instance, expressly supported a general rule requiring consumer consent for the collection and any use of their information with only limited exceptions. *Comment of Department of Veteran Affairs*, cmt. #00479, at 5. Another commenter, supporting consumer choice, emphasized the importance of offering opportunities for choice beyond a consumer's initial transaction. *Comment of Catalog Choice*, cmt. #00473, at 10-18.

167 *Comment of Center for Democracy & Technology*, cmt. #00469, at 8-11; *Comment of Consumer Federation of America*, cmt. #00358, at 6-10.

168 *Comment of Computer and Communications Industry Ass'n*, cmt. #00434, at 16; *Comment of BlueKai*, cmt. #00397, at 3-4; *Comment of Retail Industry Leaders Ass'n*, cmt. #00352, at 5-7; *U.S. Chamber of Commerce*, cmt. #00452, at 5; *Comment of National Cable & Telecommunications Ass'n*, cmt. #00432, at 23-24; *Comment of Yahoo! Inc.*, cmt. #00444, at 9-10.

169 *Comment of Phorm Inc.*, cmt. #00353, at 5; *Comment of Verizon*, cmt. #00428, at 11-13.

define specific business models. With respect to those practices that fall outside the "commonly accepted" categories, commenters also addressed the mechanics of providing choice at the relevant time and what types of practices require enhanced choice.

Consistent with the discussion and analysis set forth below, the Commission retains the proposed framework's simplified choice model. Establishing consumer choice as a baseline requirement for companies that collect and use consumer data, while also identifying certain practices where choice is unnecessary, is an appropriately balanced model. It increases consumers' control over the collection and use of their data, preserves the ability of companies to innovate new products and services, and sets clear expectations for consumers and industry alike. In order to better foster innovation and take into account new technologies and business models, however, the Commission is providing further clarification of the framework's simplified choice concept.

1. PRACTICES THAT DO NOT REQUIRE CHOICE.

Proposed Principle: Companies do not need to provide choice before collecting and using consumers' data for commonly accepted practices, such as product fulfillment.

The preliminary staff report identified five categories of data practices that companies can engage in without offering consumer choice, because they involve data collection and use that is either obvious from the context of the transaction or sufficiently accepted or necessary for public policy reasons. The categories included: (1) product and service fulfillment; (2) internal operations; (3) fraud prevention; (4) legal compliance and public purpose; and (5) first-party marketing. In response to the comments received, the Commission revises its approach to focus on the context of the consumer's interaction with a company, as discussed below.

a. General Approach to "Commonly Accepted" Practices.

While generally supporting the concept that choice is unnecessary for certain practices, a variety of commenters addressed the issue of whether the list of "commonly accepted" practices was too broad or too narrow.[170] A number of industry commenters expressed concern that the list of practice categories was too narrow and rigid. These commenters stated that, by enumerating a list of specific practices, the proposed framework created a bright-line standard that freezes in place current practices and potentially could harm innovation and restrict the development of new business models.[171] In addition, the commenters asserted that notions of what is "commonly accepted" can change over time with the development of new ways to collect or use data. They also stated that line-drawing in this context could stigmatize business practices that fall outside of the "commonly accepted" category and place companies that engage in them at a competitive

---

170 *Comment of AT&T Inc.,* cmt. #00420, at 18-22; *Comment of Center for Democracy & Technology,* cmt. #00469, at 8-11; *Comment of Consumers Union,* cmt. #00362, at 9-12; *Comment of Consumer Federation of America,* cmt. #00358, at 6-10; *Comment of National Cable & Telecommunications Ass'n,* cmt. #00432, at 23-25.

171 *Comment of Computer and Communications Industry Ass'n,* cmt. #00434, at 16; *Comment of BlueKai,* cmt. #00397, at 4; *Comment of Retail Industry Leaders Ass'n,* cmt. #00352, at 6-7; *Comment of Yahoo! Inc.,* cmt. #00444, at 9-12; *Comment of National Cable & Telecommunications Ass'n,* cmt. #00432, at 23-24.

disadvantage. To resolve these concerns, commenters called on the Commission to provide guidance on how future practices relate to the "commonly accepted" category.[172] Similarly, one commenter suggested that the practices identified in the preliminary staff report should serve as illustrative guidelines rather than an exhaustive and final list.[173]

Commenters also supported adding additional practices or clarifying that the "commonly accepted" category includes certain practices. Some industry commenters suggested, for example, expanding the concept of fraud prevention to include preventing security attacks, "phishing,"[174] and spamming or to protect intellectual property.[175] Other recommendations included adding analytical data derived from devices that are not tied to individuals, such as smart grid data used for energy conservation and geospatial data used for mapping, surveying or providing emergency services.[176] With respect to online behavioral advertising in particular, some trade associations recommended clarifying that the "commonly accepted" category of practices includes the use of IP addresses and third-party cookie data when used for purposes such as "frequency capping," "attribution measurement," and similar inventory or delivery measurements and to prevent click fraud.[177]

More generally, some commenters discussed the "repurposing" of existing consumer data to develop new products or services. For example, one company supported expanding the "internal operations" category to include the practice of product and service improvement.[178] One commenter recommended treating any uses of data that consumers would "reasonably expect under the circumstances" as commonly accepted.[179] Another noted that, whether a new use of consumer data should be considered commonly accepted would depend upon a variety of factors, including the extent to which the new use is consistent with previously defined uses.[180]

In contrast to the calls for expanding the "commonly accepted" practice categories to cover various practices, a number of consumer and privacy organizations advocated for a more restrictive approach to determining the practices that do not require consumer choice. Although agreeing that choice is not necessary for product and service fulfillment, one commenter stated that most of the other practices enumerated in the proposed framework – including internal operations, fraud prevention, and legal compliance and public purpose – were vague and required additional description. The commenter called on

---

172 *Comment of eBay*, cmt. #00374, at 6-7; *Comment of Phorm Inc.*, cmt. #00353, at 5.

173 *See Comment of AT&T Inc.*, cmt. #00420, at 18.

174 Phishing uses deceptive spam that appears to be coming from legitimate, well-known sources to trick consumers into divulging sensitive or personal information, such as credit card numbers, other financial data, or passwords.

175 *See Comment of Microsoft Corp.*, cmt. #00395, at 8 (security attacks, phishing schemes, and spamming); *Comment of Business Software Alliance*, cmt. #00389, at 5-6 (security access controls and user and employee authentication, cybercrime and fraud prevention and detection, protecting and enforcing intellectual property and trade secrets).

176 *See Comment of IBM*, cmt. #00433, at 5 (energy conservation); *Comment of Management Ass'n for Private Programming Surveyors*, cmt. #00205, at 2-3 (mapping, surveying or providing emergency services).

177 *See Comment of Online Publishers Ass'n*, cmt. #00315, at 5 (frequency capping, click fraud); *Comment of Interactive Advertising Bureau*, cmt. #00388, at 9 (attribution measurement).

178 *See Comment of AT&T Inc.*, cmt. #00420, at 18-19.

179 *See Comment of Microsoft Corp.*, cmt. #00395, at 8.

180 *See Comment of Future of Privacy Forum*, cmt. #00341, at 5.

the Commission to define these terms as narrowly as possible so that they would not become loopholes used to undermine consumer privacy.[181]

One privacy advocate expressed reservations about the breadth of the "internal operations" category of practices – specifically, the extent to which it could include product improvement and website analytics. This commenter stated that, if viewed broadly, product improvement could justify, for example, a mobile mapping application collecting precise, daily geolocation data about its customers and then retaining the data long after providing the service for which the data was necessary. Similarly, this commenter noted that companies potentially could use analytics programs to create very detailed consumer profiles to which many consumers might object, without offering them any choice. This commenter recommended that the Commission revise the proposed framework's internal operations category to make it consistent with the "operational purpose" language contained in H.R. 611 from the 112th Congress, which would include, among other things, "basic business functions such as accounting, inventory and supply chain management, quality assurance, and internal auditing."[182]

The Commission believes that for some practices, the benefits of providing choice are reduced – either because consent can be inferred or because public policy makes choice unnecessary. However, the Commission also appreciates the concerns that the preliminary staff report's definition of "commonly accepted practices" may have been both under-inclusive and over-inclusive. To the extent the proposed framework was interpreted to establish an inflexible list of specific practices, it risked undermining companies' incentives to innovate and develop new products and services to consumers, including innovative methods for reducing data collection while providing valued services. On the other hand, companies could read the definition so broadly that virtually any practice could be considered "commonly accepted."

The standard should be sufficiently flexible to allow for innovation and new business models but also should cabin the types of practices that do not require consumer choice. To strike that balance, the Commission refines the standard to focus on the *context of the interaction* between a business and the consumer. This new "context of the interaction" standard is similar to the concept suggested by some commenters that the need for choice should depend on reasonable consumer expectations,[183] but is intended to provide businesses with more concrete guidance. Rather than relying solely upon the inherently subjective test of consumer expectations, the revised standard focuses on more objective factors related to the consumer's relationship with a business. Specifically, whether a practice requires choice turns on the extent

181 *See Comment of Consumer Federation of America*, cmt. #00358, at 6.

182 *See Comment of Center for Democracy & Technology*, cmt. #00469, at 8-9 (citing BEST PRACTICES Act, H.R. 611, 112th Congress § 2(5)(iii) (2011).

183 *See Comment of Microsoft Corp.*, cmt. #00395, at 8; *Comment of National Cable & Telecommunications Ass'n*, cmt. #00432, at 23-26; *Comment of Pharmaceutical Research & Manufacturers of America*, cmt. #00477, at 13.

to which the practice is consistent with the context of the transaction or the consumer's existing relationship with the business, or is required or specifically authorized by law.[184]

The purchase of an automobile from a dealership illustrates how this standard could apply. In connection with the sale of the car, the dealership collects personal information about the consumer and his purchase. Three months later, the dealership uses the consumer's address to send him a coupon for a free oil change. Similarly, two years after the purchase, the dealership might send the consumer notice of an upcoming sale on the type of tires that came with the car or information about the new models of the car. In this transaction the data collection and subsequent use is consistent with the context of the transaction and the consumer's relationship with the car dealership. Conversely, if the dealership sells the consumer's personal information to a third-party data broker that appends it to other data in a consumer profile to sell to marketers, the practice would not be consistent with the car purchase transaction or the consumer's relationship with the dealership.

Although the Commission has revised the standard for evaluating when choice is necessary, it continues to believe that the practices highlighted in the preliminary staff report – fulfilment, fraud prevention, internal operations, legal compliance and public purpose, and most first-party marketing[185] – provide illustrative guidance regarding the types of practices that would meet the revised standard and thus would not typically require consumer choice. Further, drawing upon the recommendations of several commenters,[186] the Commission agrees that the fraud prevention category would generally cover practices designed to prevent security attacks or phishing; internal operations would encompass frequency capping and similar advertising inventory metrics; and legal compliance and public purpose would cover intellectual property protection or using location data for emergency services.[187] It should be noted, however, that even within these categories there may be practices that are inconsistent with the context of the interaction standard and thus warrant consumer choice. For instance, there may be contexts in which the "repurposing" of data to improve existing products or services would exceed the internal operations concept. Thus, where a product improvement involves additional sharing of consumer data with third parties, it would no longer be an "internal operation" consistent with the context of the consumer's interaction with a company. On the

---

184 As noted above, focusing on the context of the interaction is consistent with the Respect for Context principle in the Consumer Privacy Bill of Rights proposed by the White House. *See* White House, *Consumer Data Privacy in a Networked World: A Framework for Protecting Privacy and Promoting Innovation in the Global Digital Economy*, App. A. (Feb. 2012), *available at* http://www.whitehouse.gov/sites/default/files/privacy-final.pdf. The Respect for Context principle requires companies to limit their use of consumer data to purposes that are consistent with the company's relationship with the consumer and with the context in which the consumer disclosed the data, unless the company is legally required to do otherwise. If a company will use data for other purposes it must provide a choice at a prominent point, outside of the privacy policy.

185 *See supra* at Section IV.C.1.

186 *See supra* note 175.

187 With respect to use of geolocation data for mapping, surveying or similar purposes, if the data cannot reasonably be linked to a specific consumer, computer, or device, a company collecting or using the data would not need to provide a consumer choice mechanism. Similarly, if a company takes reasonable measures to de-identify smart grid data and takes the other steps outlined above, the company would not be obligated to obtain consent before collecting or using the data. *See supra* Section IV.A.4.

other hand, product improvements such as a website redesign or a safety improvement would be the type of "internal operation" that is generally consistent with the context of the interaction.[188]

b. First-Party Marketing Generally Does Not Require Choice, But Certain Practices Raise Special Concerns.

The preliminary staff report's questions regarding first-party marketing generated a large number of comments. As discussed, the Commission has revised the standard for determining whether a practice requires consumer choice but believes that most first-party marketing practices are consistent with the consumer's relationship with the business and thus do not necessitate consumer choice. Nevertheless, as a number of the commenters discussed, there are certain practices that raise special concerns and therefore merit additional analysis and clarification.

> (i) Companies Must Provide Consumers With A Choice Whether To Be Tracked Across Other Parties' Websites.

Commenters raised questions about companies and other services that have first-party relationships with consumers, but may have access to behavioral activity data that extends beyond the context of that first-party relationship. For example, in response to the question in the preliminary staff report regarding the use of deep packet inspection ("DPI"),[189] a number of commenters cited the ability of ISPs to use DPI to monitor and track consumers' movements across the Internet and use the data for marketing.[190] There appeared to be general consensus among the commenters that, based on the potential scope of the tracking, an ISP's use of DPI for marketing purposes is distinct from other forms of marketing practices by companies that have a first-party relationship with consumers, and thus at a minimum requires consumer choice.[191]

Similarly, commenters cited the use of "social plugins" – such as the Facebook "Like" button – that allow social media services to track consumers across every website that has installed the plugin.[192] The commenter stated that, as with DPI, consumers would not expect social media sites to track their visits to other websites or that the profiles created from such tracking could be used for marketing.

---

188 Moreover, even if a given practice does not necessitate consumer choice, the framework's other elements – *e.g.*, data collection limits and disposal requirements, increased transparency – would still apply, thereby preventing a company from exploiting these categories.

189 Deep packet inspection ("DPI") refers to the ability of ISPs to analyze the information, comprised of data packets, that traverses their networks when consumers use their services.

190 *See Comment of AT&T Inc.*, cmt. #00420, at 21-22 & n.34; *Comment of Berlin Commissioner for Data Protection & Freedom of Information*, cmt. #00484, at 2-3; *Comment of Computer & Communications Industry Ass'n*, cmt. #00434, at 15; *Comment of Phorm Inc.*, cmt. #00353, App. A at 3-4; *Comment of U.S. Public Policy Council of the Ass'n for Computing Machinery*, cmt. #00431, at 6.

191 *See Comment of Phorm Inc.*, cmt. #00353, App. A at 3-4; *Comment of Center for Democracy & Technology*, cmt. #00469, at 14-15; *Comment of AT&T Inc.*, cmt. #00420, at 21-22 & n.34.

192 *See Comment of Consumer Federation of America*, cmt. #00358, at 8 (citing Justin Brookman, *Facebook Pressed to Tackle Lingering Privacy Concerns*, Center for Democracy & Technology (June 16, 2010), *available at* https://www.cdt.org/blogs/justin-brookman/facebook-pressed-tackle-lingering-privacy-concerns); *Comment of Berkeley Center for Law & Technology*, cmt. #00347, at 8; *see also* Arnold Roosendaal, *Facebook Tracks and Traces Everyone: Like This!*, (Nov. 30, 2010), *available at* http://papers.ssrn.com/so13/papers.cfm?abstract_id=1717563 (detailing how Facebook tracks consumers through the Like button, including non-Facebook members and members who have logged out of their Facebook accounts); Nik Cubrilovic, *Logging Out Of Facebook Is Not Enough*, NEW WEB ORDER (Sept. 25, 2011), http://nikcub.appspot.com/posts/logging-out-of-facebook-is-not-enough.

The Commission agrees that where a company that has a first-party relationship with a consumer for delivery of a specific service but also tracks the consumer's activities across other parties' websites, such tracking is unlikely to be consistent with the context of the consumer's first-party relationship with the entity. Accordingly, under the final framework, such entities should not be exempt from having to provide consumers with choices. This is true whether the entity tracks consumers through the use of DPI, social plug-ins, http cookies, web beacons, or some other type of technology.[193]

As an example of how this standard can apply, consider a company with multiple lines of business, including a search engine and an ad network. A consumer has a "first-party relationship" with the company when using the search engine. While it may be consistent with this first-party relationship for the company to offer contextual ads on the search engine site, it would be inconsistent with the first-party search engine relationship for the company to use its third-party ad network to invisibly track the consumer across the Internet.

To use another example, many online retailers engage in the practice of "retargeting," in which the retailer delivers an ad to a consumer on a separate website based on the consumer's previous activity on the retailer's website.[194] Because the ad is tailored to the consumer's activity on the retailer's website, it could be argued that "retargeting" is a first-party marketing practice that does not merit consumer choice. However, because it involves tracking the consumer from the retailer's website to a separate site on which the retailer is a third party and communicating with the consumer in this new context, the Commission believes that the practice of retargeting is inconsistent with the context of consumer's first-party interaction with the retailer. Thus, where an entity has a first-party relationship with a consumer on its own website, and it engages in third-party tracking of the consumer across other websites the entity should provide meaningful choice to the consumer.

(ii) Affiliates Are Third Parties Unless The Affiliate Relationship Is Clear to Consumers.

Several trade organizations stated that first-party marketing should include the practice of data sharing among all of a particular entity's corporate affiliates and subsidiaries.[195] In contrast, a number of commenters – including individual companies and consumer advocates – took a more limited approach that would treat affiliate sharing as a first-party practice only if the affiliated companies share a trademark, are commonly-branded, or the affiliated relationship is otherwise reasonably clear to consumers.[196] One consumer advocate also suggested restricting data sharing to commonly-branded affiliates in the same line of business so that the data would be used in a manner that is consistent with the purpose for which the first party collected it.[197]

---

193 See *infra* at Section IV.C.2.d. (discussing special concerns that arise by comprehensive tracking by large platform providers).

194 For example, a consumer visits an online sporting goods retailer, looks at but does not purchase running shoes, and then visits a different website to read about the local weather forecast. A first party engages in retargeting if it delivers an ad for running shoes to the consumer on the third-party weather site.

195 *See Comment of Direct Marketing Ass'n, Inc.*, cmt. #00449, at 16; *Comment of Interactive Advertising Bureau*, cmt. #00388, at 8; *Comment of National Cable & Telecommunications Ass'n*, cmt. #00432, at 24.

196 *See Comment of Yahoo! Inc.*, cmt. #00444, at 11; *Comment of IBM*, cmt. #00433, at 6; *Comment of AT&T Inc.*, cmt. #00420, at 20; *Comment of Catalog Choice*, cmt. #00473, at 10; *Comment of Consumers Union*, cmt. #00362, at 10-11.

197 *See Comment of Consumers Union*, cmt. #00362, at 10-11.

The Commission maintains the view that affiliates are third parties, and a consumer choice mechanism is necessary unless the affiliate relationship is clear to consumers. Common branding is one way of making the affiliate relationship clear to consumers. By contrast, where an affiliate relationship is hidden – such as between an online publisher that provides content to consumers through its website and an ad network that invisibly tracks consumers' activities on the site – marketing from the affiliate would not be consistent with a transaction on, or the consumer's relationship with, that website. In this scenario consumers should receive a choice about whether to allow the ad network to collect data about their activities on the publisher's site.

(iii) Cross-Channel Marketing Is Generally Consistent with the Context of a Consumer's Interaction with a Company.

A variety of commenters also discussed the issue of whether the framework should require choice for cross-channel marketing, *e.g.*, where a consumer makes an in-store purchase and receives a coupon – not at the register, but in the mail or through a text message. These commenters stated that the framework should not require choice when a first party markets to consumers through different channels, such as the Internet, email, mobile apps, texts, or in the offline context.[198] In support of this conclusion, one commenter stated that restricting communications from a first party to the initial means of contact would impose costs on business without any consumer benefits.[199]

The Commission agrees that the first-party marketing concept should include the practice of contacting consumers across different channels. Regardless of the particular means of contact, receipt of a message from a company with which a consumer has interacted directly is likely to be consistent with the consumer's relationship with that company.[200] At the same time, as noted above, if an offline or online retailer tracks a customer's activities on a third-party website, this is unlikely to be consistent with the customer's relationship with the retailer; thus, choice should be required.

(iv) Companies Should Implement Measures to Improve The Transparency of Data Enhancement.

A large number of commenters discussed whether the practice of data enhancement, by which a company appends data obtained from third-party sources to information it collects directly from consumers, should require choice. Some of these commenters specifically objected to allowing companies to enhance data without providing consumers choice about the practice.[201]

For example, one academic organization characterized data enhancement without consumer choice as "trick[ing]" consumers into participating in their own profiling for the benefit of companies.[202] As

---

198 *See Comment of Yahoo! Inc.*, cmt. #00444, at 10; *Comment of IBM*, cmt. #00433, at 6; *Comment of AT&T Inc.*, cmt. #00420, at 20; *Comment of Catalog Choice*, cmt. #00473, at 9-10; *Comment of Direct Marketing Ass'n, Inc.*, cmt. #00449, at 16; *Comment of Interactive Advertising Bureau*, cmt. #00388, at 8.

199 *See Comment of American Catalog Mailers Ass'n,* cmt. #00424, at 7.

200 Such marketing communications would, of course, still be subject to any existing restrictions, including the CAN-SPAM Act, 15 U.S.C. §§ 7701-7713 (2010).

201 *See Comment of Consumer Federation of America*, cmt. #00358, at 10; *Comment of Consumers Union*, cmt. #00362, at 11.

202 *Comment of Berkeley Center for Law & Technology*, cmt. #00347, at 9-10.

companies develop new means for collecting data about individuals, this commenter stated, consumers should have more tools to control data collection, not fewer.[203]

Similarly, a consumer organization explained that consumers may not anticipate that the companies with which they have a relationship can obtain additional data about them from other sources, such as social networking sites, and use the data for marketing.[204] This commenter concluded that requiring companies to provide choice will necessitate better explanations of the practice, which will lead to improved consumer understanding.

Other stakeholders also raised concerns about data enhancement absent consumer choice. One company focused on the practice of enhancing online cookie data or IP addresses with offline identity data and stated that such enhancement should be subject to consumer choice.[205] In addition, a data protection authority stated that consumers are likely to expect choice where the outcome of data enhancement could negatively affect the consumer or where the sources of data used for enhancement would be unexpected to the consumer.[206]

Alternatively, a number of industry commenters opposed requiring consumer choice for data enhancement in connection with first-party marketing. These commenters described data enhancement as a routine and longstanding practice that allows businesses to better understand and serve their consumers.[207] Commenters enumerated a variety of benefits from the availability and use of third-party data, including: development of new or more relevant products and services; ensuring the accuracy of databases; reducing barriers to small firms seeking to enter markets; helping marketers identify the best places to locate retail stores; and reducing irrelevant marketing communications.[208]

One commenter noted that requiring content publishers such as newspapers to offer consumer choice before buying information from non-consumer-facing data brokers would impose logistical and financial challenges that would interfere with publishers' ability to provide relevant content or sell the advertising to support it.[209] Other commenters claimed that, where the data used for enhancement comes from third-party sources, it was likely subject to choice at the point of collection from the consumer and therefore providing additional choice is unnecessary.[210] Taking a similar approach, one company noted that the third-party source of the data should be responsible for complying with the framework when it shares data, and the recipient should be responsible for any subsequent sharing of the enhanced data.[211]

---

203 *Id.*, at 8-10 (describing Williams-Sonoma's collection of consumers' zip codes in *Pineda v. Williams-Sonoma Stores, Inc.*, 246 P.3d 612 (Cal. 2011)).

204 *Comment of Consumer Federation of America*, cmt. #00358, at 10.

205 *See Comment of Phorm Inc.*, cmt. #00353, at 5.

206 *See Comment of the Information Commissioner's Office of the UK*, cmt. #00249, at 3.

207 *See Comment of Newspaper Ass'n of America*, cmt. #00383, at 7-8; *Comment of National Cable & Telecommunications Ass'n*, cmt. #00432, at 24-26; *Comment of Experian*, cmt. #00398, at 5-6; *Comment of Magazine Publishers of America*, cmt. #00332, at 4; *Consumer Data Industry Ass'n*, cmt. #00363, at 2-3.

208 *Comment of Experian*, cmt. #00398, at 6; *see Comment of Newspaper Ass'n of America*, cmt. #00383, at 6-8.

209 *Comment of Newspaper Ass'n of America*, cmt. #00383, at 7-8.

210 *Comment of Experian*, cmt. #00398, at 9 (citing the Direct Marketing Association's Guidelines for Ethical Business Practice); *Comment of Magazine Publishers of America*, cmt. #00332, at 5-6.

211 *Comment of Microsoft Corp.*, cmt. #00395, at 8.

The issue of whether a first-party marketer should provide choice for data enhancement is particularly challenging because the practice involves two separate and distinct types of consumer data collection. One involves the consumer-to-business transfer of data – for instance, where an online retailer collects information directly from the consumer by tracking the products the consumer purchased in the store or looked at while visiting the retailer's website. The other involves a business-to-business transfer of data – such as where retailer purchases consumer data from a non-consumer-facing data broker.

As to the first type of data collection, for the reasons discussed above, if the first party does not share information with third parties or track consumers across third-party websites, the practice would be consistent with the context of the consumer's interaction with the company.[212] Therefore, the framework would not call for a consumer choice mechanism. In contrast, because the second type of data collection involves the transfer of data from one business to another and does not directly involve the consumer (and therefore is typically unknown to the consumer), it is unlikely to be consistent with a transaction or relationship between the consumer and the first party. The Commission nevertheless recognizes that it would be impractical to require the first-party marketer to offer a choice mechanism when it appends data from third-party sources to the data it collects directly from its consumers. As discussed in the comments, such a requirement would impose costs and logistical problems that could preclude the range of benefits that data enhancement facilitates.

Instead, full implementation of the framework's other components should address the privacy concerns that commenters raised about data enhancement. First, companies should incorporate privacy by design concepts, including limiting the amount of data they collect from consumers and third parties alike to accomplish a specific business purpose, reducing the amount of time they retain such data, and adopting reasonable security measures. The framework also calls for consumer choice where a company shares with a third party the data it collects from a consumer. Thus, consumers will have the ability to control the flow of their data to third parties who might sell the data to others for enhancement. In addition, companies should improve the transparency of their practices by disclosing that they engage in data enhancement and educating consumers about the practice, identifying the third-party sources of the data, and providing a link or other contact information so the consumer can contact the third-party source directly. Finally, to further protect consumer privacy, the Commission recommends that first parties that obtain marketing data for enhancement should take steps to encourage their third-party data broker sources to increase their own transparency, including by participating in a centralized data broker website, discussed further below, where consumers could learn more information about data brokers and exercise choices.[213] The first parties may also consider contractually requiring their data broker sources to take these steps.

---

212 See *supra* Section IV.C.1.b.(i).

213 The concept of such a website is discussed, *infra*, Section IV.D.2.a.

DATA ENHANCEMENT CASE STUDY:
FACIAL RECOGNITION SOFTWARE

Facial recognition technology[1] enables the identification of an individual based on his or her distinct facial characteristics. While this technology has been used in experiments for over thirty years, until recently it remained costly and limited under real world conditions.[2] However, steady improvements in the technology combined with increased computing power have shifted this technology out of the realm of science fiction and into the marketplace. As costs have decreased and accuracy improved, facial recognition software has been incorporated into a variety of commercial products. Today it can be found in online social networks and photo management software, where it is used to facilitate photo-organizing,[3] and in mobile apps where it is used to enhance gaming.[4]

This surge in the deployment of facial recognition technology will likely boost the desire of companies to use data enhancement by offering yet another means to compile and link information about an individual gathered through disparate transactions and contexts. For instance, social networks such as Facebook and LinkedIn, as well as websites like Yelp and Amazon, all encourage users to upload profile photos and make these photos publicly available. As a result, vast amounts of facial data, often linked with real names and geographic locations, have been made publicly available. A recent paper from researchers at Carnegie Mellon University illustrated how they were able to combine readily available facial recognition software with data mining algorithms and statistical re-identification techniques to determine in many cases an individual's name, location, interests, and even the first five digits of the individual's Social Security number, starting with only the individual's picture.[5]

Companies could easily replicate these results. Today, retailers use facial *detection* software in digital signs to analyze the age and gender of viewers and deliver targeted advertisements.[6] Facial detection does not uniquely identify an individual. Instead, it detects human faces and determines gender and approximate age range. In the future, digital signs and kiosks placed in supermarkets, transit stations, and college campuses could capture images of viewers and, through the use of facial *recognition* software, match those faces to online identities, and return advertisements based on the websites specific individuals have visited or the publicly available information contained in their social media profiles. Retailers could also implement loyalty programs, ask users to associate a photo with the account, then use the combined data to link the consumer to other online accounts or their in-store actions. This would enable the retailer to glean information about the consumer's purchase habits, interests, and even movements,[7] which could be used to offer discounts on particular products or otherwise market to the consumer.

The ability of facial recognition technology to identify consumers based solely on a photograph, create linkages between the offline and online world, and compile highly detailed dossiers of information, makes it especially important for companies using this technology to implement privacy by design concepts and robust choice and transparency policies. Such practices should include reducing the amount of time consumer information is retained, adopting reasonable security measures, and disclosing to consumers that the facial data they supply may be used to link them to information from third parties or publicly available sources. For example, if a digital sign uses data enhancement to deliver targeted advertisements to viewers, it should immediately delete the data after the consumer has walked away. Likewise, if a kiosk is used to invite shoppers to register for a store loyalty program, the shopper should be informed that the photo taken by the kiosk camera and associated with the account may be combined with other data to market discounts and offers to the shopper. If a company received the data from other sources, it should disclose the sources to the consumer.

NOTES

1   The Commission held a facial recognition workshop on December 8, 2011. *See* FTC Workshop, *Face Facts: A Forum on Facial Recognition Technology* (Dec. 8, 2011), http://www.ftc.gov/bcp/workshops/facefacts/.

2   *See* Alessandro Acquisti *et al.*, *Faces of Facebook: Privacy in the Age of Augmented Reality*, http://www.heinz.cmu.edu/~acquisti/face-recognition-study-FAQ/.

3   *See* Justin Mitchell, *Making Photo Tagging Easier*, THE FACEBOOK BLOG (June 30, 2011, 5:16 PM), https://blog.facebook.com/blog.php?post=467145887130; Matt Hickey, *Picasa Refresh Brings Facial Recognition*, TECHCRUNCH (Sept. 2, 2008), http://techcrunch.com/2008/09/02/picasa-refresh-brings-facial-recognition/.

4   *See* Tomio Geron, *Viewdle Launches 'Third Eye' Augmented Reality Game*, FORBES, June 22, 2011, *available at* http://www.forbes.com/sites/tomiogeron/2011/06/22/viewdle-lauches-third-eye-augmented-reality-game/.

5   *See* Alessandro Acquisti *et al.*, *Faces of Facebook: Privacy in the Age of Augmented Reality*, http://www.heinz.cmu.edu/~acquisti/face-recognition-study-FAQ/.

6   *See* Shan Li & David Sarno, *Advertisers Start Using Facial Recognition to Tailor Pitches*, L.A. TIMES, Aug. 21, 2011, *available at* http://articles.latimes.com/2011/aug/21/business/la-fi-facial-recognition-20110821.

7   For instance, many consumers use services such as Foursquare which allow them to use their mobile phone to "check in" at a restaurant to find friends who are nearby. *See* Foursquare, About Foursquare, https://foursquare.com/about.

(v) Companies Should Generally Give Consumers a Choice Before Collecting Sensitive Data for First-Party Marketing.

Commenters addressed whether companies that collect sensitive data[214] for their own marketing should offer consumer choice. A number of privacy and consumer organizations asserted that even where a business collects data in a first-party setting, any marketing based on sensitive data should require the consumer's affirmative express consent.[215] These commenters stated that the use of sensitive data for marketing could cause embarrassment for consumers or lead to various types of discriminatory conduct, including denial of benefits or being charged higher prices. One such commenter also noted that heightened choice for sensitive data is consistent with the FTC staff's Self-Regulatory Principles for Online Behavioral Advertising ("2009 OBA Report").[216]

Rather than always requiring consent, an industry trade association pushed for a more flexible approach to the use of sensitive data in first-party marketing.[217] This commenter stated that the choice analysis should depend upon the particular context and circumstances in which the data is used. The commenter noted that, for example, with respect to sensitive location data, where a consumer uses a wireless service to find nearby restaurants and receive discounts, the consumer implicitly understands his location data will be used and consent can be inferred.

The Commission agrees with the commenters who stated that affirmative express consent is appropriate when a company uses sensitive data for any marketing, whether first- or third-party. Although, as a general rule, most first-party marketing presents fewer privacy concerns, the calculus changes when the data is sensitive. Indeed, when health or children's information is involved, for example, the likelihood that data misuse could lead to embarrassment, discrimination, or other harms is increased. This risk exists regardless of whether the entity collecting and using the data is a first party or a third party that is unknown to the consumer. In light of the heightened privacy risks associated with sensitive data, first parties should provide a consumer choice mechanism at the time of data collection.[218]

At the same time, the Commission believes this requirement of affirmative express consent for first-party marketing using sensitive data should be limited. Certainly, where a company's business model is *designed to target* consumers based on sensitive data – including data about children, financial and health information, Social Security numbers, and certain geolocation data – the company should seek affirmative express consent before collecting the data from those consumers.[219] On the other hand, the risks to consumers may not justify the potential burdens on general audience businesses that *incidentally collect* and use sensitive

---

214 The Commission defines as sensitive, at a minimum, data about children, financial and health information, Social Security numbers, and certain geolocation data, as discussed below. See *infra* Section IV.C.2.e.(ii).

215 *Comment of Center for Democracy & Technology*, cmt. #00469, at 10; *Comment of Consumer Federation of America*, cmt. #00358, at 8-9; *Comment of Consumers Union*, cmt. #00362, at 12-13.

216 *See Comment of Center for Democracy & Technology*, cmt. #00469 at 10 (citing FTC, *FTC Staff Report: Self-Regulatory Principles for Online Behavioral Advertising*, 43-44 (2009), http://www.ftc.gov/os/2009/02/P085400behavadreport.pdf).

217 *Comment of CTIA – The Wireless Ass'n*, cmt. #00375, at 4-6.

218 Additional discussion regarding the necessary level of consent for the collection or use of sensitive data, as well as other practices that raise special privacy considerations, is set forth below. See *infra* Section IV.C.2.e.(ii).

219 These categories of sensitive data are discussed further below. See *infra* Section IV.C.2.e.(ii).

information. For example, the Commission has previously noted that online retailers and services such as Amazon.com and Netflix need not provide choice when making product recommendations based on prior purchases. Thus, if Amazon.com were to recommend a book related to health or financial issues based on a prior purchase on the site, it need not provide choice. However, if a health website is designed to target people with particular medical conditions, that site should seek affirmative express consent when marketing to consumers.

> **Final Principle:** Companies do not need to provide choice before collecting and using consumer data for practices that are consistent with the context of the transaction or the company's relationship with the consumer, or are required or specifically authorized by law.

2. FOR PRACTICES INCONSISTENT WITH THE CONTEXT OF THEIR INTERACTION WITH CONSUMERS, COMPANIES SHOULD GIVE CONSUMERS CHOICES.

> **Proposed Principle:** For practices requiring choice, companies should offer the choice at a time and in a context in which the consumer is making a decision about his or her data.

For those practices for which choice is contemplated, the proposed framework called on companies to provide choice at a time and in a context in which the consumer is making a decision about his or her data. In response, commenters discussed a number of issues, including the methods for providing just in time choice, when "take-it-or-leave-it" choice may be appropriate, how to respond to the call for a Do Not Track mechanism that would allow consumers to control online tracking, and the contexts in which affirmative express consent is necessary.

The Commission adopts the proposed framework's formulation that choice should be provided at a time and in a context in which the consumer is making a decision about his or her data. The Commission also adds new language addressing when a company should seek a consumer's affirmative express consent.

a. Companies Should Provide Choices At a Time and In a Context in Which the Consumer Is Making a Decision About His or Her Data.

The call for companies to provide a "just in time" choice generated numerous comments. Several consumer organizations as well as industry commenters stressed the importance of offering consumer choice at the time the consumer provides – and the company collects or uses – the data at issue and pointed to examples of existing mechanisms for providing effective choice.[220] One commenter stated that in order to make choice mechanisms meaningful to consumers, companies should incorporate them as a feature of a product or service rather than as a legal disclosure.[221] Using its vendor recommendation service as an example, this commenter suggested incorporating a user's sharing preferences into the sign-up process instead of setting such preferences as a default that users can later adjust and personalize. Another

---

220 *See Comment of Consumer Federation of America*, cmt. #00358, at 10; *Comment of Center for Democracy & Technology*, cmt. #00469, at 23-24; *Comment of AT&T Inc.*, cmt. #00420, at 22-23; *Comment of Phorm Inc.*, cmt. #00353, at 9-10.

221 *Comment of AT&T Inc.*, cmt. #00420, at 22-23.

commenter stated that choice options should occur in a "time-appropriate manner" that takes into account the "functional and aesthetic context" of the product or service.[222]

Others raised concerns about the practicality of providing choice prior to the collection or use of data in different contexts.[223] For instance, a number of commenters discussed the offline retail context and noted that cashiers are typically unqualified to communicate privacy information or to discuss data collection and use practices with customers.[224] One commenter further discussed the logistical problems with providing such information at the point of sale, citing consumer concerns about ease of transaction and in-store wait times.[225] Other commenters described the impracticality of offering and obtaining advance consent in an offline mail context, such as a magazine subscription card or catalogue request that a consumer mails to a fulfillment center.[226] In the online context, one commenter expressed concern that "pop-up" choice mechanisms complicate or clutter the user experience, which could lead to choice "fatigue."[227] Another commenter noted that where data collection occurs automatically, such as in the case of online behavioral advertising, obtaining consent before collection could be impractical.[228]

One theme that a majority of the commenters addressing this issue articulated is the need for flexibility so that companies can tailor the choice options to specific business models and contexts.[229] Rather than a rigid reliance on advance consent, commenters stated that companies should be able to provide choice before collection, close to the time of collection, or a time that is convenient to the consumer.[230] The precise method should depend upon context, the sensitivity of the data at issue, and other factors.[231] Citing its own best practices guidance, one trade organization recommended that the Commission focus not on the precise mechanism for offering choice, but on whether the consent is informed and based on sufficient notice.[232]

The Commission appreciates the concerns that commenters raised about the timing of providing choices. Indeed, the proposed framework was not intended to set forth a "one size fits all" model for designing consumer choice mechanisms. Staff instead called on companies to offer clear and concise choice

---

222 *Comment of Center for Democracy & Technology*, cmt. #00469, at 11.

223 *See Comment of Microsoft Corp.*, cmt. #00395, at 8-10, 14; *Comment of SIFMA*, cmt. #00265, at 5-6; *Comment of Retail Industry Leaders Ass'n*, cmt. #00352, at 8-10.

224 *Comment of Retail Industry Leaders Ass'n*, cmt. #00352, at 8; *Comment of Experian*, cmt. #00398, at 9.

225 *Comment of Retail Industry Leaders Ass'n*, cmt. #00352, at 8.

226 *See Comment of Magazine Publishers of America*, cmt. #00332, at 4 (noting that the "blow-in cards" in magazines often used to solicit new subscriptions have very limited space, and including lengthy disclosures on these cards could render them unreadable); *Comment of American Catalogue Mailers Ass'n*, cmt. #00424, at 7.

227 *See Comment of Retail Industry Leaders Ass'n*, cmt. #00352 at 7; *see also Comment of Experian*, cmt. #00398, at 9 (noting that the proposed changes in notice and choice procedures would be inconvenient for consumers and would damage the consumer experience).

228 *Comment of Retail Industry Leaders Ass'n*, cmt. #00352, at 8.

229 *Comment of Microsoft Corp.*, cmt. #00395, at 2; *Comment of AT&T Inc.*, cmt. #00420 at 3, 7; *Comment of Consumers Union*, cmt. #00362, at 5, 11-12; *Comment of Consumer Federation of America*, cmt. #00358, at 10.

230 *Comment of Retail Industry Leaders Ass'n*, cmt. #00352, at 9.

231 *Comment of Facebook, Inc.*, cmt. #00413, at 10; *Comment of Retail Industry Leaders Ass'n*, cmt. #00352, at 9; *see also Comment of Experian*, cmt. #00398, at 9 (generally disputing the need for "just-in-time" notice, but acknowledging that it might be justified for the transfer to non-affiliated third parties of sensitive information for marketing purposes).

232 *See Comment of CTIA - The Wireless Ass'n*, cmt. #00375, at 10 (describing the form of consent outlined in the CTIA's "Best Practices and Guidelines for Location-Based Services").

mechanisms that are easy to use and are delivered at a time and in a context that is relevant to the consumer's decision about whether to allow the data collection or use. Precisely how companies in different industries achieve these goals may differ depending on such considerations as the nature or context of the consumer's interaction with a company or the type or sensitivity of the data at issue.

In most cases, providing choice before or at the time of collection will be necessary to gain consumers' attention and ensure that the choice presented is meaningful and relevant. If a consumer is submitting his or her data online, the consumer choice could be offered, for example, directly adjacent to where the consumer is entering his or her data. In other contexts, the choice might be offered immediately upon signing up for a service, as in the case of a social networking website.

In some contexts, however, it may be more practical to communicate choices at a later point. For example, in the case of an offline retailer, the choice might be offered close to the time of a sale, but in a manner that will not unduly interfere with the transaction. This could include communicating the choice mechanism through a sales receipt or on a prominent poster at the location where the transaction takes place. In such a case, there is likely to be a delay between when the data collection takes place and when the consumer is able to contact the company in order to exercise any choice options. Accordingly, the company should wait for a disclosed period of time before engaging in the practices for which choice is being offered.[233] The Commission also encourages companies to examine the effectiveness of such choice mechanisms periodically to determine whether they are sufficiently prominent, effective, and easy to use.

Industry is well positioned to design and develop choice mechanisms that are practical for particular business models or contexts, and that also advance the fundamental goal of giving consumers the ability to make informed and meaningful decisions about their privacy. The Commission calls on industry to use the same type of creativity industry relies on to develop effective marketing campaigns and user interfaces for consumer choice mechanisms. One example of such a creative approach is the online behavioral advertising industry's development of a standardized icon and text that is embedded in targeted advertisements. The icon and text are intended to communicate that the advertising may rely on data collected about consumers. They also serve as a choice mechanism to allow the consumer to exercise control over the delivery of such ads.[234] Even though in most cases, cookie placement has already occurred, the in-ad disclosure provides a logical "teachable moment" for the consumer who is making a decision about his or her data.[235]

b. Take-it-or-Leave-it Choice for Important Products or Services Raises Concerns When Consumers Have Few Alternatives.

Several commenters addressed whether it is appropriate for a company to make a consumer's use of its product or service contingent upon the consumer's acceptance of the company's data practices. Two industry

---

233 The FTC recognizes that incorporating this delay period may require companies to make programming changes to their systems. As noted above, in the discussion of legacy data systems, see *supra* at Section IV.B.2., these changes may take time to implement.

234 As noted in Section IV.C.2.c., industry continues to consider ways to make the icon and opt out mechanism more usable and visible for consumers.

235 *But see Comment of Center for Digital Democracy and U.S. PIRG*, cmt. #00338, at 29 (criticizing visibility of the icon to consumers).

commenters suggested that "take-it-or-leave-it" or "walk away" choice is common in many business models, such as retail and software licensing, and companies have a right to limit their business to those who are willing to accept their policies.[236] Another commenter stated that preventing companies from offering take-it-or-leave-it choice might be unconstitutional under the First Amendment.[237] Other commenters, however, characterized walk away choice as generally inappropriate.[238] Some argued that the privacy framework should prevent companies from denying consumers access to goods or services, including website content, where consumers choose to limit the collection or use of their data.[239]

Most of the commenters that addressed this issue took a position somewhere in between.[240] In determining whether take-it-or-leave-it choice is appropriate, these commenters focused on three main factors. First, they noted that there must be adequate competition, so that the consumer has alternative sources to obtain the product or service in question.[241] Second, they stated that the transaction must not involve an essential product or service.[242] Third, commenters stated that the company offering take-it-or-leave-it choice must clearly and conspicuously disclose the terms of the transaction so that the consumer is able to understand the value exchange. For example, a company could clearly state that in exchange for receiving a service at "no cost," it collects certain information about your activity and sells it to third parties.[243] Expanding upon this point, commenters stressed that to ensure consumer understanding of the nature of the take-it-or-leave-it bargain, the disclosure must be prominent and not buried within a privacy policy.[244]

The Commission agrees that a "take it or leave it" approach is problematic from a privacy perspective, in markets for important services where consumers have few options.[245] For such products or services, businesses should not offer consumers a "take it or leave it" choice when collecting consumers' information in a manner inconsistent with the context of the interaction between the business and the consumer. Take,

---

236 *Comment of Performance Marketing Ass'n*, cmt. #00414, at 6; *Comment of Business Software Alliance*, cmt. #00389, at 11-12.

237 *Comment of Tech Freedom*, cmt. #00451, at 17.

238 *Comment of Consumer Federation of America*, cmt. #00358, at 11; *Comment of ePrio, Inc.*, cmt. #00267, at 4-5.

239 *Comment of Consumer Federation of America*, cmt. #00358, at 11; *see also Comment of Consumers Union*, cmt. #00362, at 12 (urging that consumers who choose to restrict sharing of their PII with unknown third parties should not be punished for that choice).

240 *See, e.g., Comment of Center for Democracy & Technology*, cmt. #00469, at 13 (stating that it has no objection to take-it-or-leave-it approaches, provided there is competition and the transaction does not involve essential services); *Comment of Microsoft Corp.*, cmt. #00395, at 10 (stating that take-it-or-leave-it choice is appropriate provided the "deal" is made clear to the consumer); *Comment of the Information Commissioner's Office of the UK*, cmt. #00249, at 4 (stating that take-it-or-leave-it choice would be inappropriate where the consumer has no real alternative but to use the service); *Comment of Reed Elsevier, Inc.*, cmt. #00430, at 11 (stating that while acceptable for the websites of private industry, websites that provide a public service and may be the single source of certain information, such as outsourced government agency websites, should not condition their use on take-it-or-leave-it terms).

241 *Comment of Center for Democracy & Technology*, cmt. #00469, at 13; *Comment of the Information Commissioner's Office of the UK*, cmt. #00249, at 4.

242 *Comment of Center for Democracy & Technology*, cmt. #00469, at 13; *Comment of Reed Elsevier, Inc.*, cmt. #00430, at 11.

243 *Comment of Microsoft Corp.*, cmt. #00395, at 10; *see also Comment of Center for Democracy & Technology*, cmt. #00469, at 13 (stating that the terms of the bargain should be clearly and conspicuously disclosed).

244 *Comment of TRUSTe*, cmt. #00450, at 11; *see also Comment of Center for Democracy & Technology*, cmt. #00469, at 13 (stating that terms should be "transparent and fairly presented").

245 This Report is not intended to reflect Commission guidance regarding Section 5's prohibition on unfair methods of competition.

for example, the purchase of an important product that has few substitutes, such as a patented medical device. If a company offered a limited warranty for the device only in exchange for the consumer's agreeing to disclose his or her income, religion, and other highly-personal information, the consumer would not have been offered a meaningful choice and a take-it-or-leave approach would be inappropriate.

Another example is the provision of broadband Internet access. As consumers shift more aspects of their daily lives to the Internet – shopping, interacting through social media, accessing news, entertainment, and information, and obtaining government services – broadband has become a critical service for many American consumers. When consumers have few options for broadband service, the take-it-or-leave-it approach becomes one-sided in favor of the service provider. In these situations, the service provider should not condition the provision of broadband on the customer's agreeing to, for example, allow the service provider to track all of the customer's online activity for marketing purposes. Consumers' privacy interests ought not to be put at risk in such one-sided transactions.

With respect to less important products and services in markets with sufficient alternatives, take-it-or-leave-it choice can be acceptable, provided that the terms of the exchange are transparent and fairly disclosed – *e.g.*, "we provide you with free content in exchange for collecting information about the websites you visit and using it to market products to you." Under the proper circumstances, such choice options may result in lower prices or other consumer benefits, as companies develop new and competing ways of monetizing their business models.

c. Businesses Should Provide a Do Not Track Mechanism To Give Consumers Control Over the Collection of Their Web Surfing Data.

Like the preliminary staff report, this report advocates the continued implementation of a universal, one-stop choice mechanism for online behavioral tracking, often referred to as Do Not Track. Such a mechanism should give consumers the ability to control the tracking of their online activities.

Many commenters discussed the progress made by industry in developing such a choice mechanism in response to the recommendations of the preliminary staff report and the 2009 OBA Report, and expressed support for these self-regulatory initiatives.[246] These initiatives include the work of the online advertising industry over the last two years to simplify disclosures and improve consumer choice mechanisms; efforts by the major browsers to offer new choice mechanisms; and a project of a technical standards body to

---

[246] *See, e.g., Comment of American Ass'n of Advertising Agencies et. al*, cmt. #00410, at 3 (describing the universal choice mechanisms used in the coalition's Self-Regulatory Principles for Online Behavioral Advertising Program); *Comment of BlueKai*, cmt. #00397, at 3 (describing its development of the NAI Opt-Out Protector for Firefox); *Comment of Computer & Communications Industry Ass'n*, cmt. #00434, at 17 (describing both company-specific and industry-wide opt-out mechanisms currently in use); *Comment of Direct Marketing Ass'n, Inc.*, cmt. #00449, at 3 (stating that the Self-Regulatory Principles for Online Behavioral Advertising Program addresses the concerns that motivate calls for a "Do-Not-Track" mechanism); *Comment of Facebook, Inc.*, cmt. #00413, at 13 (describing behavioral advertising opt-out mechanisms developed by both browser makers and the advertising industry); *Comment of Future of Privacy Forum*, cmt. #00341, at 2-4 (describing the development of a browser-based Do-Not-Track header and arguing that the combined efforts of browser companies, ad networks, consumers, and government are likely to result in superior choice mechanisms); *Comment of Google, Inc.*, cmt. #00417, at 5 (describing its Ad Preferences Manager and Keep My Opt-Outs tools); *Comment of Interactive Advertising Bureau*, cmt. #00388, at 5-7 (describing the Self-Regulatory Principles for Online Behavioral Advertising Program); *Comment of Microsoft Corp.*, cmt. #00395, at 11-14 (describing a variety of browser-based and ad network-based choice tools currently available); *Comment of U.S. Chamber of Commerce*, cmt. #00452, at 5-6 (describing a variety of browser-based and ad network-based choice tools currently available).

standardize opt outs for online tracking.[247] A number of commenters, however, expressed concerns that existing mechanisms are still insufficient. Commenters raised questions about the effectiveness and comprehensiveness of existing mechanisms for exercising choice and the legal enforceability of such mechanisms.[248] Due to these concerns, some commenters advocated for legislation mandating a Do Not Track mechanism.[249]

The Commission commends recent industry efforts to improve consumer control over behavioral tracking and looks forward to final implementation. As industry explores technical options and implements self-regulatory programs, and Congress examines Do Not Track, the Commission continues to believe that in order to be effective, any Do Not Track system should include five key principles. First, a Do Not Track system should be implemented universally to cover all parties that would track consumers. Second, the choice mechanism should be easy to find, easy to understand, and easy to use. Third, any choices offered should be persistent and should not be overridden if, for example, consumers clear their cookies or update their browsers. Fourth, a Do Not Track system should be comprehensive, effective, and enforceable. It should opt consumers out of behavioral tracking through any means and not permit technical loopholes.[250] Finally, an effective Do Not Track system should go beyond simply opting consumers out of receiving targeted advertisements; it should opt them out of collection of behavioral data for all purposes other than those that would be consistent with the context of the interaction (*e.g.*, preventing click-fraud or collecting de-identified data for analytics purposes).[251]

Early on the companies that make web browsers stepped up to the challenge to give consumers choice about how they are tracked online, sometimes known as the "browser header" approach. The browser header is transmitted to all types of entities, including advertisers, analytics companies, and researchers, that track consumers online. Just after the FTC's call for Do Not Track, Microsoft developed a system to let users of Internet Explorer prevent tracking by different companies and sites.[252] Mozilla introduced a Do Not Track privacy control for its Firefox browser that an impressive number of consumers have adopted.[253]

---

247 *See supra* at Section II.C.1.

248 *Comment of American Civil Liberties Union*, cmt. #00425, at 12; *Comment of Center for Digital Democracy and U.S. PIRG*, cmt. #00338, at 28; *Comment of Consumer Federation of America*, cmt. #00358, at 13; *Comment of Consumers Union*, cmt. #00362, at 14; *see also Comment of World Privacy Forum*, cmt. #00369, at 3 (noting prior failures of self-regulation in the online advertising industry).

249 *E.g., Comment of Consumers Union*, cmt. #00362, at 14; *Comment of World Privacy Forum*, cmt. #00369, at 3.

250 For example, consumers may believe they have opted out of tracking if they block third-party cookies on their browsers; yet they may still be tracked through Flash cookies or other mechanisms. The FTC recently brought an action against a company that told consumers they could opt out of tracking by exercising choices through their browsers; however, the company used Flash cookies for such tracking, which consumers could not opt out of through their browsers. *In the Matter of ScanScout, Inc.*, FTC Docket No. C-4344 (Dec. 21, 2011) (consent order), *available at* http://www.ftc.gov/os/caselist/1023185/111221s canscoutdo.pdf.

251 Such a mechanism should be different from the Do Not Call program in that it should not require the creation of a "Registry" of unique identifiers, which could itself cause privacy concerns.

252 *Comment of Microsoft Corp.*, cmt. #00395, at 12.

253 *Comment of Mozilla*, cmt. #00480, at 2; Alex Fowler, *Do Not Track Adoption in Firefox Mobile is 3x Higher than Desktop*, MOZILLA PRIVACY BLOG, (Nov. 2, 2011), http://blog.mozilla.com/privacy/2011/11/02/do-not-track-adoption-in-firefox-mobile-is-3x-higher-than-desktop/.

Apple subsequently included a similar Do Not Track control in Safari.[254] Google has taken a slightly different approach – providing consumers with a tool that persistently opts them out of most behavioral advertising.[255]

In another important effort, the online advertising industry, led by the DAA, has implemented a behavioral advertising opt-out program. The DAA's accomplishments are notable: it has developed a notice and choice mechanism through a standard icon in ads and on publisher sites; deployed the icon broadly, with over 900 billion impressions served each month; obtained commitments to follow the self-regulatory principles from advertisers, ad networks, and publishers that represent close to 90 percent of the online behavioral advertising market; and established an enforcement mechanism designed to ensure compliance with the principles.[256] More recently, the DAA addressed one of the long-standing criticisms of its approach – how to limit secondary use of collected data so that the consumer opt out extends beyond simply blocking targeted ads to the collection of information for other purposes. The DAA has released new principles that include limitations on the collection of tracking data and prohibitions on the use or transfer of the data for employment, credit, insurance, or health care eligibility purposes.[257] Just as important, the DAA recently moved to address some persistence and usability criticisms of its icon-based opt out by committing to honor the tracking choices consumers make through their browser settings.[258]

At the same time, the W3C Internet standards-setting body has gathered a broad range of stakeholders to create an international, industry-wide standard for Do Not Track. The group includes a wide variety of stakeholders, including DAA members; other U.S. companies; international companies; industry groups; and public-interest groups. The W3C group has done admirable work to flesh out the details required to make a Do Not Track system practical in both desktop and mobile settings. The group has issued two public working drafts of its standards. Some important details remain to be filled in, and the Commission encourages all of the stakeholders to work within the W3C group to resolve these issues.

While more work remains to be done on Do Not Track, the Commission believes that the developments to date are significant and provide an effective path forward. The advertising industry, through the DAA, has committed to deploy browser-based technologies for consumer control over online tracking, alongside its ubiquitous icon program. The W3C process, thanks in part to the ongoing participation of DAA member companies, has made substantial progress toward specifying a consensus consumer choice system for tracking

---

254 Nick Wingfield, *Apple Adds Do-Not-Track Tool to New Browser*, WALL ST. J. Apr. 13, 2011, *available at* http://online.wsj.com/article/SB10001424052748703551304576261272308358858.html.

255 *Comment of Google Inc.*, cmt. #00417, at 5.

256 Peter Kosmala, *Yes, Johnny Can Benefit From Transparency & Control*, SELF-REGULATORY PROGRAM FOR ONLINE BEHAVIORAL ADVERTISING, http://www.aboutads.info/blog/yes-johnny-can-benefit-transparency-and-control (Nov. 3, 2011); *see also* Press Release, Digital Advertising Alliance, White House, DOC and FTC Commend DAA's Self-Regulatory Program to Protect Consumers Online Privacy, (Feb. 23, 2012), *available at* http://www.aboutads.info/resource/download/DAA%20White%20House%20Event.pdf.

257 Digital Advertising Alliance, *About Self-Regulatory Principles for Multi-Site Data* (Nov. 2011), *available at* http://www.aboutads.info/resource/download/Multi-Site-Data-Principles.pdf.

258 Press Release, Digital Advertising Alliance, DAA Position on Browser Based Choice Mechanism (Feb. 22, 2012), *available at* http://www.aboutads.info/resource/download/DAA.Commitment.pdf.

that is practical and technically feasible.[259] The Commission anticipates continued progress in this area as the DAA members and other key stakeholders continue discussions within the W3C process to work to reach consensus on a Do Not Track system in the coming months.

d. Large Platform Providers That Can Comprehensively Collect Data Across the Internet Present Special Concerns.

As discussed above, even if a company has a first-party relationship with a consumer in one setting, this does not imply that the company can track the consumer for purposes inconsistent with the context of the interaction across the Internet, without providing choice. This principle applies fully to large platform providers such as ISPs, operating systems, and browsers, who have very broad access to a user's online activities.

For example, the preliminary staff report sought comment on the use of DPI for marketing purposes. Many commenters highlighted the comprehensive nature of DPI.[260] Because of the pervasive tracking that DPI allows, these commenters stated that its use for marketing should require consumers' affirmative express consent.[261] Privacy concerns led one commenter to urge the Commission to oppose DPI and hold workshops and hearings on the issue.[262] Another commenter argued that a lack of significant competition among broadband providers argues in favor of heightened requirements for consumer choice before ISPs can use DPI for marketing purposes.[263]

Two major ISPs emphasized that they do not use DPI for marketing purposes and would not do so without first seeking their customers' affirmative express consent.[264] They cautioned against singling out DPI as a practice that presents unique privacy concerns, arguing that doing so would unfairly favor certain technologies or business models at the expense of others. One commenter also stated that the framework should not favor companies that use other means of tracking consumers.[265] This commenter noted that various technologies – including cookies – allow companies to collect and use information in amounts similar to that made possible through DPI, and the framework's principles should apply consistently based

---

259 A system practical for both businesses and consumers would include, for users who choose to enable Do Not Track, significant controls on the collection and use of tracking data by third parties, with limited exceptions such as security and frequency capping. As noted above, first-party sharing with third parties is not consistent with the context of the interaction and would be subject to choice. Do Not Track is one way for users to express this choice.

260 *Comment of Computer and Communications Industry Ass'n*, cmt. #00233, at 15; *Comment of Center for Democracy & Technology*, cmt. #00469, at 14-15.

261 *See Comment of Center for Democracy & Technology*, cmt. #00469, at 14; *Comment of Phorm Inc.*, cmt. #00353, at 5; *see also Comment of Computer and Communications Industry Ass'n*, cmt. #00233, at 15 (urging that heightened requirements for consumer choice apply for the use of DPI); *Comment of Online Trust Alliance*, cmt. #00299, at 6 ("The use of DPI and related technologies may also be permissible when consumers have the ability to opt-in and receive appropriate and proportional quantifiable benefits in return.")

262 *Comment of Center for Digital Democracy and U.S. PIRG*, cmt. #00338, at 37.

263 *Comment of Computer and Communications Industry Ass'n*, cmt. #00233, at 15.

264 *Comment of AT&T Inc.*, cmt. #00420, at 21; *see also Comment of Verizon*, cmt. #00428, at 7 n.6. Likewise, a trade association of telecommunications companies represented that ISPs have not been extensively involved in online behavioral advertising. *See Comment of National Cable & Telecommunications Ass'n*, cmt. #00432, at 33.

265 *See Comment of Verizon*, cmt. #00428, at 7.

on the type of information collected and how it is used.[266] Rather than isolating a specific technology, commenters urged the Commission to focus on the type of data collected and how it is used.[267]

ISPs serve as a major gateway to the Internet with access to vast amounts of unencrypted data that their customers send or receive over the ISP's network. ISPs are thus in a position to develop highly detailed and comprehensive profiles of their customers – and to do so in a manner that may be completely invisible. In addition, it may be difficult for some consumers to obtain alternative sources of broadband Internet access, and they may be inhibited from switching broadband providers for reasons such as inconvenience or expense. Accordingly, the Commission has strong concerns about the use of DPI for purposes inconsistent with an ISP's interaction with a consumer, without express affirmative consent or more robust protection.[268]

At the same time, the Commission agrees that any privacy framework should be technology neutral. ISPs are just one type of large platform provider that may have access to all or nearly all of a consumer's online activity. Like ISPs, operating systems and browsers may be in a position to track all, or virtually all, of a consumer's online activity to create highly detailed profiles.[269] Consumers, moreover, might have limited ability to block or control such tracking except by changing their operating system or browser.[270] Thus, comprehensive tracking by any such large platform provider may raise serious privacy concerns.

The Commission also recognizes that the use of cookies and social widgets to track consumers across unrelated websites may create similar privacy issues.[271] However, while companies such as Google and Facebook are expanding their reach rapidly, they currently are not so widespread that they could track a consumer's every movement across the Internet.[272] Accordingly, although tracking by these entities warrants consumer choice, the Commission does not believe that such tracking currently raises the same level of privacy concerns as those entities that can comprehensively track all or virtually of a consumer's online activity.

These are complex and rapidly evolving areas, and more work should be done to learn about the practices of all large platform providers, their technical capabilities with respect to consumer data, and their current and expected uses of such data. Accordingly, Commission staff will host a workshop in the second half

---

266 *Id.* at 7-8.

267 *See, e.g.*, *Comment of Internet Commerce Coalition*, cmt. #00447, at 10; *Comment of KINDSIGHT*, cmt. #00344, at 7-8 ; *Comment of National Cable & Telecommunications Ass'n*, cmt. #00432, at 36; *Comment of Verizon*, cmt. #00428, at 7-8.

268 This discussion does not apply to ISPs' use of DPI for network management, security, or other purposes consistent with the context of a consumer's interaction with their ISP.

269 This discussion is not meant to imply that ISPs, operating systems, or browsers are currently building these profiles for marketing purposes.

270 ISPs, operating systems, and browsers have different access to users' online activity. A residential ISP can access unencrypted traffic from all devices currently located in the home. An operating system or browser, on the other hand, can access all traffic regardless of location and encryption, but only from devices on which the operating system or browser is installed. Desktop users have the ability to change browsers to avoid monitoring, but mobile users have fewer browser options.

271 A social widget is a button, box, or other possibly interactive display associated with a social network that is embedded into another party's website.

272 BrightEdge, *Social Share Report: Social Adoption Among Top Websites*, 3-4 (July 2011), *available at* http://www.brightedge. com/resfiles/brightedge-report-socialshare-2011-07.pdf (reporting that by mid-2011, the Facebook Like button appeared on almost 11% of top websites' front pages and Google's +1 button appeared on 4.5% of top websites' front pages); *see also* Justin Osofsky, *After f8: Personalized Social Plugins Now on 100,000+ Sites*, FACEBOOK DEVELOPER BLOG (May 11, 2010, 9:15 AM), http://developers.facebook.com/blog/post/382/.

of 2012 to explore the privacy issues raised by the collection and use of consumer information by a broad range of large platform providers such as ISPs, operating systems, browsers, search engines, and social media platforms as well as how competition issues may bear on appropriate privacy protection.[273]

e. Practices Requiring Affirmative Express Consent.

Numerous commenters focused on whether certain data collection and use practices warrant a heightened level of consent – *i.e.*, affirmative express consent.[274] These practices include (1) making material retroactive changes to a company's privacy representations; and (2) collection of sensitive data. These comments and the Commission's analysis are discussed here.

(i) Companies Should Obtain Affirmative Express Consent Before Making Material Retroactive Changes To Privacy Representations.

The preliminary staff report reaffirmed the Commission's bedrock principle that companies should provide prominent disclosures and obtain affirmative express consent before using data in a manner materially different than claimed at the time of collection.[275]

Although many commenters supported the affirmative express consent standard for material retroactive changes,[276] some companies called for an opt-out approach for material retroactive changes, particularly for changes that provide benefits to consumers.[277] One example cited was the development of Netflix's personalized video recommendation feature using information that Netflix originally collected in order to send consumers the videos they requested.[278] Other companies sought to scale the affirmative consent requirement according to the sensitivity of the data and whether the data is personally identifiable.[279] Many commenters sought clarification on when a change is material – for example, whether a change in data retention periods would be a material change requiring heightened consent.[280] One company posited

---

273 *See Comment of Center for Digital Democracy and U.S. PIRG*, cmt. #00338, at 37 (recommending FTC hold a workshop to address DPI).

274 Companies may seek "affirmative express consent" from consumers by presenting them with a clear and prominent disclosure, followed by the ability to opt in to the practice being described. Thus, for example, requiring the consumer to scroll through a ten-page disclosure and click on an "I accept" button would not constitute affirmative express consent.

275 In the preliminary report, this principle appeared under the heading of "transparency." *See, e.g.*, *In the Matter of Gateway Learning Corp.*, FTC Docket No. C-4120 (Sept. 10, 2004) (consent order) (alleging that Gateway violated the FTC Act by applying material changes to a privacy policy retroactively), *available at* http://www.ftc.gov/os/caselist/0423047/040917 do0423047.pdf; *see also* FTC, *Self-Regulatory Principles for Online Behavioral Advertising* (Feb. 2009), *available at* http://www. ftc.gov/os/2009/02/P085400behavadreport.pdf (noting the requirement that companies obtain affirmative express consent before making material retroactive changes to their privacy policies).

276 *See Comment of Consumers Union*, cmt. #00362, at 17; *Comment of Future of Privacy Forum*, cmt. #00341, at 5; *Comment of Privacy Rights Clearinghouse*, cmt. #00351, at 21.

277 *See Comment of Facebook, Inc.*, cmt. #00413, at 11; *see also Comment of Retail Industry Leaders Ass'n*, cmt. #00352, at 12; *Comment of AT&T Inc.*, cmt. #00420, at 29-30; *Comment of National Cable & Telecommunications Ass'n*, cmt. #00432, at 30-31.

278 *Comment of Facebook, Inc.*, cmt. #00413, at 8.

279 *See Comment of AT&T Inc.*, cmt. #00420, at 30; *Comment of Phorm Inc.*, cmt. #00353, at 1.

280 *See Comment of Future of Privacy Forum*, cmt. #00341, at 4; *Comment of Retail Industry Leaders Ass'n*, cmt. #00352, at 12; *Comment of Microsoft Corp.*, cmt. #00395, at 17.

that the affirmative express consent standard would encourage vague disclosures at the outset to avoid the requirement for obtaining such consent.[281]

The Commission reaffirms its commitment to requiring companies to give prominent disclosures and to obtain express affirmative consent for material retroactive changes. Indeed, the Commission recently confirmed this approach in its settlements with Google and Facebook. The settlement agreements mandate that the companies give their users clear and prominent notice and obtain affirmative express consent prior to making certain material retroactive changes to their privacy practices.[282]

In response to the request for clarification on what constitutes a material change, the Commission notes that, at a minimum, sharing consumer information with third parties after committing at the time of collection not to share the data would constitute a material change. There may be other circumstances in which a change would be material, which would have to be determined on a case-by-case basis, analyzing the context of the consumer's interaction with the business.

The Commission further notes that commenters' concerns that the affirmative express consent requirement would encourage vague disclosures at the outset should be addressed by other elements of the framework. For example, other elements of the framework call on companies to improve and standardize their privacy statements so that consumers can easily glean and compare information about various companies' data practices. The framework also calls on companies to give consumers specific information and choice at a time and in a context that is meaningful to consumers. These elements, taken together, are intended to result in disclosures that are specific enough to be meaningful to consumers.

The preliminary staff report posed a question about the appropriate level of consent for prospective changes to companies' data collection and use. One commenter cited the rollout of Twitter's new user interface – "new Twitter" – as a positive example of a set of prospective changes about which consumers received ample and adequate notice and ability to exercise choice.[283] When "new Twitter" was introduced, consumers were given the opportunity to switch to or try out the new interface, or to keep their traditional Twitter profile. The Commission supports innovative efforts such as these to provide consumers with meaningful choices when a company proposes to change its privacy practices on a prospective basis.

> (ii) Companies Should Obtain Consumers' Affirmative Express Consent Before Collecting Sensitive Data.

A variety of commenters discussed how to delineate which types of data should be considered sensitive. These comments reflect a general consensus that information about children, financial and health information, Social Security numbers, and precise, individualized geolocation data is sensitive and

---

281 *Comment of Facebook, Inc.*, cmt. #00413, at 10.

282 *See In the Matter of Google Inc.*, FTC Docket No. C-4336 (Oct. 13, 2011) (consent order), *available at* http://www.ftc.gov/os/caselist/1023136/111024googlebuzzdo.pdf; *In the Matter of Facebook, Inc.*, FTC File No. 092-3184 (Nov. 29, 2011) (proposed consent order), *available at* http://www.ftc.gov/os/caselist/0923184/111129facebookagree.pdf.

283 *Comment of Electronic Frontier Foundation*, cmt. #00400, at 15.

merits heightened consent methods.[284] In addition, some commenters suggested that information related to race, religious beliefs, ethnicity, or sexual orientation, as well as biometric and genetic data, constitute sensitive data.[285] One commenter also characterized as sensitive information about consumers' online communications or reading and viewing habits.[286] Other commenters, however, noted the inherent subjectivity of the question and one raised concerns about the effects on market research if the definition of sensitive data is construed too broadly.[287]

Several commenters focused on the collection and use of information from teens, an audience that may be particularly vulnerable. A diverse coalition of consumer advocates and others supported heightened protections for teens between the ages of 13 and 17.[288] These commenters noted that while teens are heavy Internet users, they often fail to comprehend the long-term consequences of sharing their personal data. In order to better protect this audience, the commenters suggested, for example, limiting the amount of data that websites aimed at teens can collect or restricting the ability of teens to share their data widely through social media services.

Conversely, a number of industry representatives and privacy advocates objected to the establishment of different rules for teens.[289] These commenters cited the practical difficulties of age verification and the potential that content providers will simply elect to bar teen audiences.[290] Rather than requiring different choice mechanisms for this group, one company encouraged the FTC to explore educational efforts to address issues that are unique to teens.[291]

Given the general consensus regarding information about children, financial and health information, Social Security numbers, and precise geolocation data, the Commission agrees that these categories of information are sensitive. Accordingly, before collecting such data, companies should first obtain affirmative express consent from consumers. As explained above, the Commission also believes that companies should

---

284 *See, e.g., Comment of Consumer Federation of America*, cmt. #00358, at 9; *Comment of CNIL*, cmt. #00298, at 4; *Comment of Massachusetts Office of the Attorney General*, cmt. #00429, at 3; *Comment of Kindsight*, cmt. #00344, at 11; *Comment of Experian*, cmt. #00398, at 9; *Comment of Center for Democracy & Technology*, cmt. #00469, at 14; *Comment of Office of the Information and Privacy Commissioner of Ontario*, cmt. #00239, at 2; *see also Comment of TRUSTe*, cmt. #00450, at 11 (agreeing that sensitive information should be defined to include information about children, financial and medical information, and precise geolocation information but urging that sensitive information be more broadly defined as "information whose unauthorized disclosure or use can cause financial, physical, or reputational harm"); *Comment of Facebook, Inc.*, cmt. #00413, at 23 (agreeing that sensitive information may warrant enhanced consent, but noting that enhanced consent may not be possible for activities such as the posting of status updates by users where those updates may include sensitive information such as references to an illness or medical condition).

285 *See Comment of Consumer Federation of America*, cmt. #00358, at 9; *see also Comment of CNIL*, cmt. #00298, at 4, *Comment of Center for Digital Democracy and U.S. PIRG*, cmt. #00338, at 35.

286 *See Comment of Electronic Frontier Foundation*, cmt. #00400, at 7.

287 *See Comment of Marketing Research Ass'n*, cmt. #00405, at 6-7; *Comment of American Trucking Ass'ns*, cmt. #00368, at 2-3; *Comment of Microsoft Corp.*, cmt. #00395, at 10.

288 *See Comment of Institute for Public Representation*, cmt. #00346, at 4; *Comment of Consumers Union*, cmt. #00362, at 13.

289 *See Comment of Center for Democracy & Technology*, cmt. #00469, at 15; *Comment of CTIA – The Wireless Ass'n*, cmt. #00375, at 12-13; *Comment of Microsoft Corp.*, cmt. #00395, at 10; *see also Comment of Electronic Frontier Foundation*, cmt. #00400, at 14 (opposing the creation of special rules giving parents access to data collected about their teenaged children); *Comment of PrivacyActivism*, cmt. #00407, at 4 (opposing the creation of special rules giving parents access to data collected about their teenaged children).

290 *See Comment of Center for Democracy & Technology*, cmt. #00469, at 15; *Comment of CTIA – The Wireless Ass'n*, cmt. #00375, at 12-13; *Comment of Microsoft Corp.*, cmt. #00395, at 10.

291 *See Comment of Microsoft Corp.*, cmt. #00395, at 10.

follow this practice irrespective of whether they use the sensitive data for first-party marketing or share it with third parties.[292]

The Commission is cognizant, however, that whether a particular piece of data is sensitive may lie in the "eye of the beholder" and may depend upon a number of subjective considerations. In order to minimize the potential of collecting any data – whether generally recognized as sensitive or not – in ways that consumers do not want, companies should implement *all* of the framework's components. In particular, a consumer's ability to access – and in appropriate cases to correct or delete – data will allow the consumer to protect herself when she believes the data is sensitive but others may disagree.

With respect to whether information about teens is sensitive, despite the difficulties of age verification and other concerns cited in the comments, the Commission agrees that companies that target teens should consider additional protections. Although affirmative express consent may not be necessary in every advertising campaign directed to teens, other protections may be appropriate. For example, all companies should consider shorter retention periods for teens' data.

In addition, the Commission believes that social networking sites should consider implementing more privacy-protective default settings for teens. While some teens may circumvent these protections, they can function as an effective "speed bump" for this audience and, at the same time, provide an opportunity to better educate teens about the consequences of sharing their personal information. The Commission also supports access and deletion rights for teens, as discussed below.[293]

> **Final Principle:** For practices requiring choice, companies should offer the choice at a time and in a context in which the consumer is making a decision about his or her data. Companies should obtain affirmative express consent before (1) using consumer data in a materially different manner than claimed when the data was collected; or (2) collecting sensitive data for certain purposes.

D. TRANSPARENCY

> **Baseline Principle:** Companies should increase the transparency of their data practices.

Citing consumers' lack of awareness of how, and for what purposes, companies collect, use, and share data, the preliminary staff report called on companies to improve the transparency of their data practices. Commission staff outlined a number of measures to achieve this goal. One key proposal, discussed in the previous section, is to present choices to consumers in a prominent, relevant, and easily accessible place at a time and in a context when it matters to them. In addition, Commission staff called on industry to make privacy statements clearer, shorter, and more standardized; give consumers reasonable access to their data; and undertake consumer education efforts to improve consumers' understanding of how companies collect, use, and share their data.

---

292 *See infra* at Section IV.C.1.b.(v).
293 *See infra* at Section IV.D.2.b.

Commenters offered proposals for how to achieve greater transparency and sought clarification on how they should implement these elements of the framework. Although the Commission adopts the proposed framework's transparency principle without change, it clarifies the application of the framework in response to these comments, as discussed below.

1. PRIVACY NOTICES

Proposed Principle: Privacy notices should be clearer, shorter, and more standardized to enable better comprehension and comparison of privacy practices.

The preliminary staff report highlighted the consensus among roundtable participants that most privacy policies are generally ineffective for informing consumers about a company's data practices because they are too long, are difficult to comprehend, and lack uniformity.[294] While acknowledging privacy policies' current deficiencies, many roundtable participants agreed that the policies still have value – they provide an important accountability function by educating consumer advocates, regulators, the media, and other interested parties about the companies' data practices.[295] Accordingly, Commission staff called on companies to provide clear and concise descriptions of their data collection and use practices. Staff further called on companies to standardize the format and the terminology used in privacy statements so that consumers can compare the data practices of different companies and exercise choices based on privacy concerns, thereby encouraging companies to compete on privacy.

Despite the consensus from the roundtables that privacy statements are not effective at communicating a company's data collection and use practices to consumers, one commenter disagreed that privacy notices need to be improved.[296] Another commenter pointed out that providing more granular information about data collection and use practices could actually increase consumer confusion by overloading the consumer with information.[297] Other industry commenters highlighted the work they have undertaken since the preliminary staff report to improve their own privacy statements.[298]

Many consumer groups supported staff's call to standardize the format and terminology used in privacy statements so that consumers could more easily compare the practices of different companies.[299] Some commenters suggested a "nutrition label" approach for standardizing the format of privacy policies and cited

---

294 Recent research and surveys suggests that many consumers (particularly among lower income brackets and education levels) do not read or understand privacy policies, thus further heightening the need to make them more comprehensible. Notably, in a survey conducted by Zogby International, 93% of adults – and 81% of teens – indicated they would take more time to read terms and conditions for websites if they were shorter and written in clearer language. *See Comment of Common Sense Media*, cmt. #00457, at 1.

295 *See Comment of AT&T , Inc.*, cmt. #00420, at 17; *Comment of Center for Democracy & Technology*, cmt. #00469, at 24.

296 *See Comment of National Cable & Telecommunications Ass'n*, cmt. #00432, at 22.

297 *See Comment of United States Council for International Business*, cmt. #00366, at 3.

298 *See Comment of Google Inc.*, cmt. #00417, at 1; *Comment of Facebook, Inc.*, cmt. #00413, at 9; *Comment of AT&T Inc.*, cmt. #00420, at 24.

299 *See Comment of Privacy Rights Clearinghouse*, cmt. #00351, at 15-16; *Comment of Consumer Federation of America*, cmt. #00358, at 16; *Comment of Consumer Watchdog*, cmt. #00402, at 2.

research underway in this area.[300] Another suggested the "form builder" approach used for GLBA Short Notices to standardize the format of privacy notices outside the financial context.[301] One consumer group called for standardization of specific terms like "affiliate" and "anonymize" so that companies' descriptions of their data practices are more meaningful.[302] A wide range of commenters suggested that different industry sectors come together to develop standard privacy notices.[303] Other commenters opposed the idea of mandated standardized notices, arguing that the Commission should require only that privacy statements be clear and in plain language. These commenters stated that privacy statements need to take into account differences among business models and industry sectors.[304]

Privacy statements should account for variations in business models across different industry sectors, and prescribing a rigid format for use across all sectors is not appropriate. Nevertheless, the Commission believes that privacy statements should contain some standardized elements, such as format and terminology, to allow consumers to compare the privacy practices of different companies and to encourage companies to compete on privacy. Accordingly, Commission calls on industry sectors to come together to develop standard formats and terminology for privacy statements applicable to their particular industries. The Department of Commerce will convene multi-stakeholder groups to work on privacy issues; this could be a useful venue in which industry sectors could begin the exercise of developing more standardized, streamlined privacy policies.

Machine-readable policies,[305] icons, and other alternative forms of providing notice also show promise as tools to give consumers the ability to compare privacy practices among different companies.[306] In response to the preliminary staff report's question on machine-readable policies, commenters agreed that such policies could improve transparency.[307] One commenter proposed combining the use of machine-readable policies with icons and standardized policy statements (*e.g.*, "we collect but do not share consumer data

---

300 *See Comment of Consumer Watchdog*, cmt. #00402, at 2; *Comment of Consumer Federation of America*, cmt. #00358, at 16; *see also Comment of Lorrie Faith Cranor*, cmt. #00453, at 2 n.7 (discussing P3P authorizing tools that enable automatic generation of "nutrition label" privacy notices).

301 *See Comment of Privacy Rights Clearinghouse*, cmt. #00351, at 16.

302 *See Comment of Electronic Frontier Foundation*, cmt. #00400, at 6.

303 *See Comment of General Electric*, cmt. #00392, at 2; *Comment of the Information Commissioner's Office of the UK*, cmt. #00249, at 4; *Comment of Consumers Union*, cmt. #00362, at 15-16; *Comment of Facebook, Inc.*, cmt. #00413, at 9.

304 *See Comment of AT&T Inc.*, cmt. #00420, at 25; *Comment of eBay*, cmt. #00374, at 10; *Comment of National Cable & Telecommunications Ass'n*, cmt. #00432, at 29; *Comment of Retail Industry Leaders Ass'n*, cmt. #00352, at 12; *Comment of Microsoft Corp.*, cmt. #00395, at 15.

305 A machine-readable privacy policy is a statement about a website's privacy practices – such as the collection and use of data – written in a standard computer language (not English text) that software tools such as consumer's web browser can read automatically. For example, when the browser reads a machine-readable policy, the browser can compare the policy to the consumer's browser privacy preferences, and can inform the consumer when these preferences do not match the practices of the website he is visiting. If the consumer decides he does not want to visit websites that sell information to third parties, he might set up a rule that recognizes that policy and blocks such sites or display a warning upon visiting such a site. Machine-readable language will be the subject of an upcoming summit. *See* White House, National Archives & Records Administration, *Informing Consumers Through Smart Disclosures* (Mar. 1, 2012), *available at* http://www.nist.gov/ineap/ upload/Summit_Invitation_to_Agencies_FINAL.pdf (describing upcoming summit).

306 Likewise, new tools like privacyscore.com may help consumers more readily compare websites' data practices. *See* Tanzina Vega, *A New Tool in Protecting Online Privacy*, N.Y. Times, Feb. 12, 2012, *available at* http://mediadecoder.blogs.nytimes. com/2012/02/12/a-new-tool-in-protecting-online-privacy/?scp=2&sq=privacy&st=cse.

307 *Comment of Phorm Inc.*, cmt. #00353, at 9; *Comment of Lorrie Faith Cranor*, cmt. #00453, at 6.

with third parties") to simplify privacy decision-making for consumers.[308] Other commenters described how icons work or might work in different business contexts. One browser company described efforts underway to develop icons that might be used to convey information, such as whether a consumer's data is sold or may be subject to secondary uses, in a variety of business contexts.[309] Representatives from online behavioral advertising industry groups also described their steps in developing and implementing an icon to communicate that online behavioral advertising may be taking place.[310]

Commenters also discussed the particular challenges associated with providing notice in the mobile context, noting the value of icons, summaries, FAQs, and videos.[311] Indeed, some work already has been done in this area to increase the transparency of data practices. For example, the advocacy organization Common Sense Media reviews and rates mobile apps based on a variety of factors including privacy[312] and a platform provider uses an icon to signal to consumers when a mobile application is using location information.[313] In addition, CTIA – a wireless industry trade group – in conjunction with the Entertainment Software Rating Board, recently announced plans to release a new rating system for mobile apps.[314] This rating system, which is based on the video game industry's model, will use icons to indicate whether specific apps are appropriate for "all ages," "teen," or only "adult" audiences. The icons will also detail whether the app shares consumers' personal information. Noting the complexity of the mobile ecosystem, which includes device manufacturers, operating system providers, mobile application developers, and wireless carriers, some commenters called for public workshops to bring together different stakeholders to develop a uniform approach to icons and other methods of providing notice.[315] Also, as noted above, the Mobile Marketing Association has released its Mobile Application Privacy Policy.[316]

The Commission appreciates the complexities of the mobile environment, given the multitude of different entities that want to collect and use consumer data and the small space available for disclosures

---

308 *Comment of Lorrie Faith Cranor*, cmt. #00453, at 6 (explaining how icons combined with standard policies might work: "For example, a type I policy might commit to not collecting sensitive categories of information and not sharing personal data except with a company's agents, while a type II policy might allow collection of sensitive information but still commit to not sharing them, a type III policy might share non-identified information for behavioral advertising, and so on. Companies would choose which policy type to commit to. They could advertise their policy type with an associated standard icon, while also providing a more detailed policy. Users would be able to quickly determine the policy for the companies they interact with.").

309 *Comment of Mozilla*, cmt. #00480, at 12.

310 *Comment of American Ass'n of Advertising Agencies, American Advertising Federation, Ass'n of National Advertisers, Direct Marketing Ass'n, Inc., and Interactive Advertising Bureau*, cmt. #00410 at 2-3; *Comment of Digital Marketing Alliance*, cmt. #00449, at 18-24; *Comment of Evidon*, cmt. #00391, at 3-6; *Comment of Internet Advertising Bureau*, cmt. #00388, at 4.

311 *Comment of General Electric*, cmt. #00392, at 1-2; *Comment of CTIA - The Wireless Ass'n*, cmt. #00375, at 2-3; *Comment of Mozilla*, cmt. #00480, at 12.

312 *See* Common Sense Media, App Reviews, http://www.commonsensemedia.org/app-reviews.

313 *See* Letter from Bruce Sewell, General Counsel & Senior Vice President of Legal and Governmental Affairs, Apple, to Hon. Edward J. Markey, U.S. House of Representatives (May 6, 2011), *available at* http://robert.accettura.com/wp-content/uploads/2011/05/apple_letter_to_ejm_05.06.11.pdf.

314 *See* Press Release, CTIA – The Wireless Ass'n, CTIA – The Wireless Ass'n to Announce Mobile Application Rating System with ESRB (Nov. 21, 2011), *available at* http://www.ctia.org/media/press/body.cfm/prid/2145.

315 *Comment of Consumer Federation of America*, cmt. #00358, at 16; *Comment of GSMA*, cmt. #00336, at 10.

316 Although this effort is promising, more work remains. The Mobile Marketing Association's guidelines are not mandatory and there is little recourse against companies who elect not to follow them. More generally, there are too few players in the mobile ecosystem who are committed to self-regulatory principles and providing meaningful disclosures and choices.

on mobile screens. These factors increase the urgency for the companies providing mobile services to come together and develop standard notices, icons, and other means that the range of businesses can use to communicate with consumers in a consistent and clear way.

To address this issue, the Commission notes that it is currently engaged in a project to update its existing business guidance about online advertising disclosures.[317] In conjunction with this project, Commission staff will host a workshop later this year.[318] One of the topics to be addressed is mobile privacy disclosures: How can these disclosures be short, effective, and accessible to consumers on small screens? The Commission hopes that the discussions at the workshop will spur further industry self-regulation in this area.

Final Principle: Privacy notices should be clearer, shorter, and more standardized to enable better comprehension and comparison of privacy practices.

2. ACCESS

Proposed Principle: Companies should provide reasonable access to the consumer data they maintain; the extent of access should be proportionate to the sensitivity of the data and the nature of its use.

There was broad agreement among a range of commenters that consumers should have some form of access to their data. Many of these commenters called for flexibility, however, and requested that access rights be tiered according to the sensitivity and intended use of the data at issue.[319] One commenter argued that access rights should be limited to sensitive data, such as financial account information, because a broader access right would be too costly for offline retailers.[320] Some companies and industry representatives supported providing consumers full access to data that is used to deny benefits; several commenters affirmed the significance of the FCRA in providing access to information used for critical decisionmaking. For other less sensitive data, such as marketing data, they supported giving consumers a general notice describing the types of data they collect and the ability to suppress use of the data for future marketing.[321]

One commenter raised concerns about granting access and correction rights to data files used to prevent fraudulent activity, noting that such rights would create risks of fraud and identity theft. This commenter also stated that companies would need to add sensitive identifying information to their marketing databases in order to authenticate a consumer's request for information, and that the integration of multiple databases would raise additional privacy and security risks.[322]

---

317 *See* Press Release, FTC, FTC Seeks Input to Revising its Guidance to Business About Disclosures in Online Advertising (May 26, 2011), *available at* http://www.ftc.gov/opa/2011/05/dotcom.shtm.

318 *See* Press Release, FTC, FTC Will Host Public Workshop to Explore Advertising Disclosures in Online and Mobile Media on May 30, 2012 (Feb. 29, 2012), *available at* http://www.ftc.gov/opa/2012/02/dotcom.shtm.

319 *Comment of Intuit, Inc.*, cmt. #00348, at 12; *Comment of eBay*, cmt. #00374, at 10; *Comment of IBM*, cmt. #00433, at 3; *Comment of Consumers Union*, cmt. #00362, at 16.

320 *Comment of Meijer*, cmt. #00416, at 7.

321 *Comment of Intel Corp.*, cmt. #00246, at 8; *Comment of The Centre for Information Policy Leadership at Hunton & Williams LLP*, cmt. #00360, at 8; *Comment of Experian*, cmt. #00398, at 11.

322 *Comment of Experian*, cmt. #00398, at 10-11.

A number of commenters raised issues about the costs associated with providing access. One company suggested that access rights be flexible, taking into account the company's existing data infrastructure.[323] Others argued that access be granted only to consumer information that is "reasonably accessible in the course of business"[324] and one commenter said that companies should be able to charge for providing access where there are costs associated with retrieving and presenting data.[325]

Commenters also asserted that companies should tell consumers the entities with which their data has been shared.[326] Citing California's "Shine the Light" law, one commenter stated that companies should not only identify the third parties with which they share consumer data but should also disclose how the third parties use the data for marketing.[327] Another commenter pointed out that many marketers do not maintain records about data sold to other companies on an individual basis. Thus, marketers have the ability to identify the companies to which they have sold consumer data in general, but not the third parties with which they may have shared the information about any individual consumer.[328]

Some comments reflect support for requiring companies to identify for consumers the sources of data collected about them so that consumers can correct erroneous data at the source, if appropriate.[329] One commenter noted that the DMA self-regulatory guidelines currently require that a marketer identify the sources of data maintained about consumers.[330]

The Commission agrees with the commenters who stated that consumer access should be proportional to the sensitivity and the intended use of the data at issue. Indeed, the comments generally support treating access in accordance with three categories that reflect different levels of data sensitivity: (1) entities that maintain data for marketing purposes; (2) entities subject to the FCRA; and (3) entities that may maintain data for other, non-marketing purposes that fall outside of the FCRA.

At one side of the spectrum are companies that maintain data for marketing purposes. For data used solely for marketing purposes, the Commission agrees with the commenters who stated that the costs of providing individualized access and correction rights would likely outweigh the benefits. The Commission continues to support the idea of businesses providing consumers with access to a list of the categories of consumer data they hold, and the ability to suppress the use of such data for marketing. This approach

---

323 *Comment of AT&T Inc.*, cmt. #00420, at 28-29.

324 *Comment of CTIA - The Wireless Ass'n*, cmt. #00375, at 3; *Comment of Yahoo!, Inc.*, cmt. #00444, at 20; *Comment of The Centre for Information Policy Leadership at Hunton & Williams LLP*, cmt. #00360, at 5-6.

325 *Comment of U.S. Council for International Business*, cmt. #00366, at 3.

326 *Comment of Catalog Choice*, cmt. #00473, at 8-9; *Comment of the Information Commissioner's Office of the UK*, cmt. #00249, at 5.

327 *See Comment of Catalog Choice*, cmt. #00473, at 20. Under this law, businesses, upon request, must provide their customers, free of charge and within 30 days: (1) a list of the categories of personal information disclosed by the business to third parties for the third parties' marketing purposes, (2) the names and addresses of all of the third parties that received personal information from the business in the preceding calendar year, (3) and if the nature of the third parties's business cannot reasonably be determined from the third parties' name, examples of the products or services marketed by the third party. Cal. Civ. Code § 1798.83.

328 *Comment of The Centre for Information Policy Leadership at Hunton & Williams, LLP*, cmt. #00360, at 7.

329 *Comment of Reputation.com, Inc.*, cmt. #00385, at 11-12; *see also Comment of Center for Democracy & Technology*, cmt. #00469, at 25.

330 *Comment of The Centre for Information Policy Leadership at Hunton & Williams, LLP*, cmt. #00360, at 7.

will provide consumers with an important transparency tool without imposing significant new costs for businesses.[331]

The Commission does, however, encourage companies that maintain consumer data for marketing purposes to provide more individualized access when feasible. One example of an innovation in this area is the advertising preference managers that companies such as Google and Yahoo! have implemented. Yahoo!, for example, offers consumers, through its Ad Interest Manager, the ability to access the specific interest categories that Yahoo! associates with individual consumers and allows them to suppress marketing based on some or all of these categories. Using this service, an elementary school teacher who conducted online research for pet food during the time she owned a dog, but continues to receive advertisements for dog food, could remove herself from the "Consumer Packaged Goods > Pets and Animals > Food and Supplies" category while still opting to remain part of the "Life Stages > Education > K to 12" category.[332] The Commission supports efforts by companies to provide consumers with these types of granular choices to give them greater control over the marketing materials and solicitations they receive.

At the other end of the spectrum are companies that assemble and evaluate consumer information for use by creditors, employers, insurance companies, landlords, and other entities involved in eligibility decisions affecting consumers. The preliminary staff report cited the FCRA as an important tool that provides consumers with the right to access their own data that has been used to make such decisions, and if it is erroneous, to correct it. Several commenters echoed this view.[333]

The FCRA recognizes the sensitivity of the data that consumer reporting agencies maintain and the ways in which various entities use it to evaluate whether a consumer is able to participate in so many activities central to modern life; therefore, it provides consumers with access and correction rights for information contained in consumer reports. Pursuant to the FCRA, consumer reporting agencies are required to disclose to consumers, upon request, all items in the consumer's file, no matter how or where they are stored, as well as the entities with which the consumer reporting agency shared the information in a consumer's report. When consumers identify information in their report that is incomplete or inaccurate, and report it to a consumer reporting agency, the agency must investigate and correct or delete such information in certain circumstances.

As more and more consumer data becomes available from a variety of sources, companies are increasingly finding new opportunities to compile, package, and sell that information. In some instances, companies could be compiling and selling this data to those who are making decisions about a consumer's eligibility for credit, insurance, employment, and the like. To the extent companies are assembling data and marketing or selling it for such purposes, they are subject to the FCRA. For example, companies that compile social media information and provide it to employers for use in making hiring decisions are consumer reporting

---

331 As discussed above, in most cases the framework does not require companies to provide consumer choice for first-party marketing, although first parties may choose to provide such choice to meet consumer demand. Outside of the first-party marketing context, however, companies should provide consumers with the ability to suppress the use of their data for marketing.

332 *See* Yahoo!, Ad Interest Manager, http://info.yahoo.com/privacy/us/yahoo/opt_out/targeting.

333 *Comment of Consumer Data Industry Ass'n*, cmt. #00363, at 4 - 5; *Comment of Experian*, cmt. #00398, at 10.

agencies and thus required to provide consumers with access and correction rights under the FCRA.[334] These companies would also be required to inform employers about their FCRA obligation to provide adverse action notices when, for example, employment is denied.

Even if a company is not compiling and sharing data for the specific purpose of making employment, credit, or insurance eligibility decisions, if the company has reason to believe the data will be used for such purposes, it would still be covered by the FCRA. For example, recently, the Commission issued warning letters to the developers of mobile apps that compiled public record information on individuals and created apps for the purposes of learning information about friends, co-workers, neighbors, or potential suitors.[335] The Commission noted that if these apps marketed their services for employment purposes or otherwise had reason to believe that they were being used for employment purposes, the FCRA requirements would apply.

Finally, some businesses may maintain and use consumer data for purposes that do not fall neatly within either the FCRA or marketing categories discussed above. These businesses may encompass a diverse range of industry sectors. They may include businesses selling fraud prevention or risk management services, in order to verify the identities of customers. They may also include general search engines, media publications, or social networking sites. They may include debt collectors trying to collect a debt. They may also include companies collecting data about how likely a consumer is to take his or her medication, for use by health care providers in developing treatment plans.[336]

For these entities, the Commission supports the sliding scale approach, which several commenters endorsed,[337] with the consumer's ability to access his or her own data scaled to the use and sensitivity of the data. At a minimum, these entities should offer consumers access to (1) the types of information the companies maintain about them;[338] and (2) the sources of such information.[339] The Commission believes that requiring companies to identify data sources would help consumers to correct erroneous information at the source. In appropriate circumstances the Commission urges companies to provide the names of the third parties with whom consumer information is shared.

In instances where data is more sensitive or may affect benefits, more individualized notice, access, and correction rights may be warranted. For example, if a company denies services to a consumer because it could not verify the consumer's identity, it may be appropriate for the company to disclose the name of the identity verification service used. This will allow the consumer to contact the data source, which can then provide the consumer with access to the underlying information, as well as any appropriate remedies, such

---

334 15 U.S.C. §§ 1681g-1681h. *See* Letter from Maneesha Mithal, Assoc. Dir., Div. of Privacy and Identity Prot., FTC, to Renee Jackson, Counsel for Social Intelligence Corp., (May 9, 2011) (closing letter), *available at* http://www.ftc.gov/os/closings/110509socialintelligenceletter.pdf .

335 *See* Press Release, FTC, FTC Warns Marketers That Mobile Apps May Violate Fair Credit Reporting Act (Feb. 7, 2012), *available at* http://www.ftc.gov/opa/2012/02/mobileapps.shtm (describing warning letters sent by the FTC to Everify, Inc., InfoPay, Inc., and Intelligator, Inc. on Jan. 25, 2012).

336 *See* Laura Landro, *Many Pills, Many Not Taken*, WALL ST. J., Oct. 10, 2011, *available at* http://online.wsj.com/article/SB10001424052970203388804576616882856318782.html.

337 *Comment of Consumers Union*, cmt. #00362, at 16; *Comment of CTIA – The Wireless Ass'n*, cmt. #00375, at 7; *Comment of Microsoft Corp.*, cmt. #00395, at 15-16.

338 *Comment of Retail Industry Leaders Ass'n*, cmt. #00352, at Ex. A.

339 *Comment of Reputation.com, Inc.*, cmt. #00385, at 11-12. Of course, First Amendment protections would apply to journalists' sources, among other things, and the Commission's recommendations are not intended to apply in that area.

as the ability to correct the information.[340] To ensure that the consumer knows that she has been denied a benefit based on her own data, as a best practice the company should notify the consumer of the denial and the information on which the denial was based.

Verifying the identity of users who seek access to their own information is an important consideration and should be approached from a risk management perspective, focusing on the likelihood of and potential harm from misidentification. Indeed, in the example of identity verification services described above, one would not want a criminal to be able to "correct" his or her own truthful data, and it would be appropriate to require somewhat more stringent safeguards and proof of identity before allowing access and correction. Certainly, consumer reporting agencies have developed procedures allowing them to verify the identity of requesting consumers using the multiple pieces of information they have about consumers to match information provided by the requesting consumer. Companies engaged in providing data for making eligibility determinations should develop best practices for authenticating consumers for access purposes.

On the other hand, the significantly reduced risks associated with providing the wrong person's information contained in a marketing database that contains no sensitive information may justify less stringent authentication procedures.[341] As with other issues discussed in this Report, reasonableness should be the touchstone: the degree of authentication employed should be tied to the sensitivity of the information maintained and how such information is used.

a. Special Access Mechanism for Data Brokers

Data brokers are companies that collect information, including personal information about consumers, from a wide variety of sources for the purpose of reselling such information to their customers for various purposes, including verifying an individual's identity, differentiating records, marketing products, and preventing financial fraud. Several commenters noted the lack of transparency about the practices of these entities, which often have a wealth of information about consumers but never interact directly with them.[342] Consumers are often unaware of the existence of these entities, as well as the purposes for which they collect and use data.[343] One commenter noted that data brokers may sell data to employers, background screeners, and law enforcement, among others, without the consumer's knowledge.[344] The Commission has monitored data brokers since the 1990s, hosting workshops, drafting reports, and testifying before Congress about

---

340 As noted above, companies should pay close attention to the types of eligibility determinations being made to ensure they comply with the FCRA, if warranted.

341 One commenter noted that when organizations collect and maintain sensitive information about individuals, such as for banking or issuance of credit, they will ask for authenticating information before an individual can access those records. This same commenter then stated that organizations holding less sensitive data may not require similarly rigorous authentication. *See Comment of The Centre for Information Policy Leadership at Hunton & Williams, LLP*, cmt. #00360, at 7 n.6.

342 *See Comment of Privacy Rights Clearinghouse*, cmt. #00351, at 3; *Comment of Consumers Union*, cmt. #00362, at 11.

343 *See Comment of Consumer Federation of America*, cmt. #00358, at 17.

344 *See Comment of Privacy Rights Clearinghouse,* cmt. #00351, at 8.

the privacy implications of data brokers' practices.[345] Following a Commission workshop, the data broker industry created the Individual References Services Group (IRSG), a self-regulatory organization for certain data brokers.[346] Although industry ultimately terminated this organization, a series of public breaches – including one involving ChoicePoint – led to renewed scrutiny of the practices of data brokers.[347] And, indeed, there have been few broad-based efforts to implement self-regulation in this area in the recent past.

The access rights discussed above will help to improve the transparency of companies' data practices generally, whether or not they have a direct consumer interface. Because most data brokers are invisible to consumers, however, the Commission makes two additional recommendations as to these entities.

First, since 2009, the Commission has supported legislation giving access rights to consumers for information held by data brokers. During the 111th Congress, the House approved a bill that included provisions to establish a procedure for consumers to access information held by data brokers.[348] To improve the transparency of this industry's practices, the Commission has testified in support of the goals of this legislation[349] and continues to support legislation in this area.[350]

Second, the Commission recommends that the data broker industry explore the idea of creating a centralized website where data brokers that compile and sell data for marketing could identify themselves to consumers and describe how they collect consumer data and disclose the types of companies to which they sell the information. Additionally, data brokers could use the website to explain the access rights and other choices they offer consumers, and could offer links to their own sites where consumers could exercise such options.[351] This website will improve transparency and give consumers control over the data practices of companies that maintain and share data about them for marketing purposes. It can also provide consumer-facing entities such as retailers a means for ensuring that the information brokers from which they purchase "enhancement" information have instituted appropriate transparency and control mechanisms. Indeed, the

---

345 *See, e.g.,* Prepared Statement of the FTC, *Identity Theft: Recent Developments Involving the Security of Sensitive Consumer Information: Hearing Before the Senate Comm. on Banking, Housing, and Urban Affairs,* 109th Cong. (Mar. 10, 2005), *available at* http://www.ftc.gov/os/testimony/050310idtheft.pdf; *see also* FTC Workshop, *The Information Marketplace: Merging & Exchanging Consumer Data* (Mar. 13, 2001), *available at* http://www.ftc.gov/bcp/workshops/infomktplace/index. shtml; FTC Workshop, *Information Flows: The Costs and Benefits to Consumers and Businesses of the Collection and Use of Consumer Information* (June 18, 2003), *available at* http://www.ftc.gov/bcp/workshops/infoflows/030618agenda.shtm.

346 *See* FTC, *Individual Reference Services, A Report to Congress* (1997), *available at* http://www.ftc.gov/bcp/privacy/wkshp97/ irsdoc1.htm.

347 *See* Prepared Statement of the FTC, *Protecting Consumers' Data: Policy Issues Raised by ChoicePoint: Hearing before H. Comm. on Energy and Commerce, Subcomm. on Commerce, Trade, and Consumer Protection, Comm. on Energy and Commerce,* 109th Cong. (Mar. 15, 2005), *available at* http://www.ftc.gov/os/2005/03/050315protectingconsumerdata.pdf.

348 Data Accountability and Trust Act, H.R. 2221, 111th Congress (as passed by House, Dec. 8, 2009).

349 *See, e.g.,* Prepared Statement of the FTC, *Legislative Hearing on H.R. 2221, the Data Accountability and Protection Act, and H.R. 1319, the Informed P2P User Act: Hearing Before the H. Comm. on Energy and Commerce, Subcomm. on Commerce, Trade, and Consumer Protection,* 111th Cong. (May 5, 2009), *available at* http://www.ftc.gov/os/2009/05/ P064504peertopeertestimony.pdf.

350 *See, e.g.,* Prepared Statement of the FTC, *Data Security: Hearing Before the H. Comm. on Energy and Commerce, Subcomm. on Commerce, Manufacturing, and Trade,* 112th Cong. (May 4, 2011), *available at* http://www.ftc.gov/opa/2011/05/ pdf/110504datasecurityhouse.pdf; Prepared Statement of the FTC, *Data Security: Hearing Before the H. Comm. on Energy and Commerce, Subcomm. on Commerce, Manufacturing, and Trade,* 112th Cong.(June 15, 2011), *available at* http://www.ftc. gov/os/testimony/110615datasecurityhouse.pdf; Prepared Statement of the FTC, *Protecting Consumers in the Modern World: Hearing Before the S. Comm. on Commerce, Science, and Transportation,* 112th Cong. (June 29, 2011), *available at* http://www. ftc.gov/os/testimony/110629privacytestimonybrill.pdf.

351 *See Comment of World Privacy Forum,* cmt. #00376, at 6; *Comment of Consumer Federation of America,* cmt. #00358, at 17-18.

consumer-facing entities could provide consumers with a link to the centralized mechanism, after having made sure that the data brokers from which they buy data participate in such a system. The Commission will discuss with relevant industry members how this mechanism could be developed and implemented voluntarily, in order to increase the transparency of their data practices and give consumers tools to opt out.[352]

b. Access to Teen Data

One commenter proposed that teens be given regular access to whether and how their data has been shared because of their particular vulnerability to ubiquitous marketing messages and heavy use of social media and mobile devices.[353] Others noted that teens in particular may not appreciate the persistence and future effects of data that they post about themselves online and thus need a "right to be forgotten." In its comment, the French Data Protection authority advocated the "right to be forgotten," which would allow consumers to withdraw data posted online about themselves at any point, for all users, but noted in particular the need to have control over information posted in one's youth.[354] In the United States, legislation has been introduced that would give teens an eraser button, which would allow them to erase certain material on social networking sites.[355]

The Commission generally supports exploration of the idea of an "eraser button," through which people can delete content that they post online. Many companies already offer this type of feature,[356] which is consistent with the principles of data access and suppression. Such an "eraser button" could be particularly useful for teens who might not appreciate the long-term consequences of their data sharing. Teens tend to be more impulsive than adults[357] and, as a result, may voluntarily disclose more information online than they should, leaving them vulnerable to identity theft or adversely affecting potential employment or college admissions opportunities. In supporting an eraser button concept, the Commission notes that such a feature

---

352 The current website of the Direct Marketing Association (DMA) offers an instructive model for such a mechanism. The DMA – which consists of data brokers, retailers, and others – currently offers a service through which consumers can opt out of receiving marketing solicitations via particular channels, such as direct mail, from DMA member companies. *See* DMAChoice, http://www.dmachoice.org/dma/member/home.action.

353 *See Comment of Consumers Union*, cmt. #00362, at 13; *see also Center for Digital Democracy and U.S. PIRG*, cmt. #00338, at 39.

354 *Comment of CNIL*, cmt. #00298, at 3.

355 Do Not Track Kids Act of 2011, H.R. 1895, 112th Congress (2011).

356 *See* Facebook, How Do I Remove a Wall Post or Story?, *available at* http://www.facebook.com/help/?page=174851209237562; LinkedIn, Privacy Policy, http://www.linkedin.com/static?key=privacy_policy.

357 *See, e.g.*, FTC, *Transcript of March 17, 2010, Privacy Roundtable, Panel 3: Addressing Sensitive Information*, 208-215, *available at* http://www.ftc.gov/bcp/workshops/privacyrountables/PrivacyRoundtable_March2010_Transcript.pdf; *see also* Chris Hoofnagle, Jennifer King, Su Li, & Joseph Turow, *How Different Are Young Adults from Older Adults When It Comes to Information Privacy Attitudes & Policies?* (Apr. 14, 2010), *available at* http://papers.ssrn.com/sol3/papers.cfm?abstract_id=1589864.

would have to be carefully crafted in order to avoid implicating First Amendment concerns.[358] It would also need to be technically feasible and proportional to the nature, sensitivity, and amount of data collected.

Final Principle: Companies should provide reasonable access to the consumer data they maintain; the extent of access should be proportionate to the sensitivity of the data and the nature of its use.

3. CONSUMER EDUCATION

Proposed Principle: All stakeholders should expand their efforts to educate consumers about commercial data privacy practices.

In its preliminary report, FTC staff called for all stakeholders to accelerate their efforts to raise consumer awareness about data practices and to provide additional transparency tools to consumers. Staff pointed out that consumers need more education about the privacy implications of various data practices so that they can make informed decisions about the trade-offs involved. Staff posed questions about how the range of interested stakeholders – companies, industry associations, consumer groups, and government – can do a better job of informing consumers about privacy. Many commenters expressed general support for the notion that consumer education is a vital component of improving privacy protections for consumers.[359] One commenter suggested that businesses use their creative talents to make privacy more accessible for consumers, and as support, pointed to its own privacy game.[360] The game teaches players about privacy by inviting them to tour a virtual small town in which the buildings represent different parts of the commenter's privacy policy.

Over the last few years, a number of other companies and industry and consumer groups have stepped up their efforts to educate consumers about privacy and their privacy choices.[361] The Commission encourages more such efforts, with an eye toward developing clear and accessible messages that consumers will see and understand.

---

358 While consumers should be able to delete much of the information they place on a particular social media site, there may be First Amendment constraints to requiring third parties to delete the same information. In the FTC's recent proposed settlement with Facebook, the company agreed to implement measures designed to prevent any third party from accessing information under Facebook's control within a reasonable time period, not to exceed thirty days, from the time the user has deleted such information. *See In the Matter of Facebook, Inc.,* FTC File No. 092 3184 (Nov. 29, 2011) (proposed consent order), *available at* http://ftc.gov/os/caselist/0923184/111129facebookagree.pdf.

359 *See, e.g., Comment of Intuit Inc.,* cmt. #00348, at 12; *Comment of AT&T Inc.,* cmt. #00420, at 30-31; *Comment of Consumers Union,* cmt. #00362, at 18.

360 *Comment of Zynga Inc.,* cmt. #00459, at 4.

361 *See, e.g.,* Common Sense Media, App Reviews, http://www.commonsensemedia.org/app-reviews (listing reviews that evaluate privacy and safety concerns posed by common mobile applications designed for children); Google, Ad Preferences, Frequently Asked Questions, http://www.google.com/ads/preferences/html/faq.html; Interactive Advertising Bureau, Privacy Matters Campaign, http://www.iab.net/privacymatters/campaign.php; Kashmir Hill, *Zynga's PrivacyVille – It's Not Fun, But It Gets the Job Done,* FORBES, July 8, 2011, *available at* http://www.forbes.com/sites/kashmirhill/2011/07/08/zyngas-privacyville-its-not-fun-but-it-gets-the-job-done/.

A range of commenters suggested that the FTC explicitly endorse or sponsor various private sector-led consumer education efforts.[362] The Commission certainly supports private sector education efforts, and encourages private sector entities to freely use the FTC's extensive consumer and business education materials, under their own branding.

For example, the FTC encourages businesses to use information from its OnGuardOnline.gov website, which aims to help people be safe, secure and responsible online. The OnGuardOnline.gov campaign is a partnership of 15 federal agencies. The site includes articles, videos, games and tutorials to teach home users, small businesses or corporate employees about privacy-related topics like using Wi-Fi networks, peer-to-peer file sharing, mobile apps, and online tracking. The OnGuard Online Blog provides the latest cybersecurity news and practical tips from the FTC and other federal agencies. The FTC publishes this blog regularly and encourages companies to copy and disseminate it. Additionally, the FTC has continued its own consumer education efforts in the privacy area. Over the last year, the Commission released consumer education materials on a variety of topics including: using Wi-Fi hot spots; managing browser and "Flash" cookies; understanding mobile privacy; and protecting against child identity theft.[363]

> **Final Principle:** All stakeholders should expand their efforts to educate consumers about commercial data privacy practices.

V. CONCLUSION

The final privacy framework set forth in this Report reflects the extensive record developed through the Commission's privacy roundtables as well as the over 450 public comments received in response to the proposed framework issued in December of 2010. The FTC recommends that Congress consider baseline privacy legislation while industry implements the final privacy framework through individual company initiatives and through strong and enforceable self-regulatory initiatives. As discussed throughout the report, there are a number of specific areas where policy makers have a role in assisting with the implementation of the self-regulatory principles that make up the privacy framework. Areas where the FTC will be active over the course of the next year include the following.

- ◆ **Do Not Track:** As discussed above, industry has made significant progress in implementing Do Not Track. The browser vendors have developed tools that consumers can use to signal that they do not want to be tracked; the DAA has developed its own icon-based tool and has committed to honor the browser tools; and the W3C has made substantial progress in creating an international standard for Do Not Track. However, the work is not done. The Commission will work with these groups to complete implementation of an easy-to use, persistent, and effective Do Not Track system.

---

362 *Comment of United States Council for International Business*, cmt. #00366, at 4; *Comment of IMS Health*, cmt. #00380, at 5; *Comment of The Privacy Projects*, cmt. #00482, at 2-3.

363 FTC, *Wise Up About Wi-Fi: Tips for Using Public Wireless Networks* (2011), http://www.ftc.gov/bcp/edu/pubs/consumer/alerts/alt193.shtm; FTC, *Cookies: Leaving a Trail on the Web*, http://onguardonline.gov/articles/0042-cookies-leaving-trail-web; FTC, *Understanding Mobile Apps*, http://onguardonline.gov/articles/0018-understanding-mobile-apps; FTC Workshop, *Stolen Futures: A Forum on Child Identity Theft*, (July 12, 2011), http://www.ftc.gov/bcp/workshops/stolenfutures/.

- **Mobile:** The Commission calls on companies providing mobile services to work toward improved privacy protections, including the development of short, meaningful disclosures. To this end, FTC staff has initiated a project to update its business guidance about online advertising disclosures.[364] As part of this project, staff will host a workshop on May 30, 2012 and will address, among other issues, mobile privacy disclosures and how these disclosures can be short, effective, and accessible to consumers on small screens. The Commission hopes that the workshop will spur further industry self-regulation in this area.

- **Data Brokers:** To address the invisibility of, and consumers' lack of control over, data brokers' collection and use of consumer information, the Commission supports targeted legislation – similar to that contained in several of the data security bills introduced in the 112th Congress – that would provide consumers with access to information about them held by a data broker.[365] To further increase transparency, the Commission calls on data brokers that compile data for marketing purposes to explore creating a centralized website where data brokers could (1) identify themselves to consumers and describe how they collect and use consumer data and (2) detail the access rights and other choices they provide with respect to the consumer data they maintain.

- **Large Platform Providers:** To the extent that large platforms, such as Internet Service Providers, operating systems, browsers, and social media, seek to comprehensively track consumers' online activities, it raises heightened privacy concerns. To further explore privacy and other issues related to this type of comprehensive tracking, FTC staff intends to host a public workshop in the second half of 2012.

- **Promoting enforceable self-regulatory codes:** The Department of Commerce, with the support of key industry stakeholders, is undertaking a project to facilitate the development of sector-specific codes of conduct. FTC staff will participate in that project. To the extent that strong privacy codes are developed, the Commission will view adherence to such codes favorably in connection with its law enforcement work. The Commission will also continue to enforce the FTC Act to take action against companies that engage in unfair or deceptive practices, including the failure to abide by self-regulatory programs they join.

In all other areas, the Commission calls on individual companies, trade associations, and self-regulatory bodies to adopt the principles contained in the privacy framework, to the extent they have not already done so. For its part, the FTC will focus its policy efforts on the five areas identified above, vigorously enforce existing laws, work with industry on self-regulation, and continue to target its education efforts on building awareness of existing data collection and use practices and the tools to control them.

---

364 *See* Press Release, FTC, FTC Seeks Input to Revising its Guidance to Businesses About Disclosures in Online Advertising (May 26, 2011), *available at* http://www.ftc.gov/opa/2011/05/dotcom.shtm.

365 *See* Data Accountability and Trust Act, H.R. 1707, 112th Congress (2011); Data Accountability and Trust Act of 2011, H.R. 1841, 112th Congress (2011); Data Security and Breach Notification Act of 2011, S. 1207, 112th Congress (2011).

FTC Privacy Milestones

FTC Privacy Milestones

Laws & Rules   Workshops
Cases   Education
Reports

1970	Fair Credit Reporting Act enacted
1972	First Fair Credit Reporting Act (FCRA) case: In the Matter of Credit Bureau of Lorain
1975	FTC sues tax preparer for improperly using customers' information to market its loans: FTC v. Beneficial Corporation
1970s	FTC brings 15 additional enforcement actions against credit bureaus and report users
1983	First FCRA case against a nationwide credit bureau: FTC v. TransUnion
1985	FCRA sweep against users of consumer reports
1990	Commission staff issues comprehensive commentary on the FCRA
1991	FTC sues TRW for FCRA violations: FTC v. TRW
1992	FCRA sweep against employers using credit reports
1995	FTC sues Equifax for FCRA violations: In the Matter of Equifax Credit Information Services
1996	First major revision of the Fair Credit Reporting Act
	FTC sponsors workshop: *Consumer Privacy on the Global Information Infrastructure*
1997	First spam case: FTC v. Nia Cano
	FTC hosts traveling workshops to discuss revisions of FCRA
	FTC sponsors workshop: *Consumer Information Privacy*
	FTC issues *Individual Reference Services: A Federal Trade Commission Report to Congress*
1998	FTC issues *Privacy Online: A Federal Trade Commission Report to Congress*
1999	First case involving children's privacy: In the Matter of Liberty Financial
	First consumer privacy case: In the Matter of GeoCities
	FTC issues *Self-Regulation and Privacy Online: A Federal Trade Commission Report to Congress*
	FTC sponsors workshop: *Online Profiling*
	FTC launches ID Theft website: consumer.gov/idtheft and ID Theft Online Complaint Form
	FTC's 877-ID-THEFT consumer helpline established
2000	Children's Online Privacy Protection Rule (COPPA) goes into effect
	Gramm-Leach-Bliley Financial Privacy Rule goes into effect
	Three nationwide consumer reporting agencies pay $2.5 million in civil penalties for FCRA violations: US v. Equifax Credit Information Services, US v. TransUnion, and US v. Experian Information Solutions
	First COPPA case: FTC v. Toysmart.com
	FTC issues *Online Profiling: A Federal Trade Commission Report to Congress*
	FTC issues *Privacy Online: Fair Information Practices in the Electronic Marketplace: A Federal Trade Commission Report to Congress*

FTC Privacy Milestones

continued

	FTC sponsors workshop: *The Mobile Wireless Web, Data Services and Beyond: Emerging Technologies and Consumer Issues*
	FTC publishes ID Theft booklet for victims: *When Bad Things Happen to Your Good Name*
2001	COPPA Safe Harbor Program begins
	First civil penalty cases under COPPA: <u>US v. Looksmart</u>, <u>US v. Monarch Services</u>, <u>US v. Bigmailbox</u>
	FTC sponsors workshops: *The Information Marketplace: Merging and Exchanging Consumer Data*; *Gramm-Leach-Bliley Educational Program on Financial Privacy*; and *Get Noticed: Effective Financial Privacy Notices: An Interagency Workshop*
	FTC publishes ID Theft Affidavit
2002	First data security case: <u>In the Matter of Eli Lilly & Company</u>
	FTC settles data security charges related to Microsoft's Passport service: <u>In the Matter of Microsoft</u>
	FTC sponsors workshop: *Consumer Information Security Workshop*
	FTC issues report on *Public Workshop: The Mobile Wireless Web, Data Services and Beyond: Emerging Technologies and Consumer Issues*
	FTC launches 10-minute educational ID Theft video
	FTC distributes over 1 million ID Theft booklets for victims
2003	Fair and Accurate Credit Transactions Act (FACTA) passed
	National Do Not Call Registry goes into effect
	Gramm-Leach-Bliley Safeguards Rule goes into effect
	FTC sues companies for sharing students' survey data with commercial marketers: <u>In the Matter of Education Research Center of America and Student Marketing Group</u>
	Guess settles FTC data security charges: <u>In the Matter of Guess?</u>
	FTC issues *Technologies for Protecting Personal Information: A Staff Workshop Report*
	FTC sponsors workshops: *Technologies for Protecting Personal Information*; *Spam Forum*; and *Costs and Benefits Related To the Collection and Use of Consumer Information*
2004	CAN-SPAM Rule goes into effect
	CAN-SPAM Adult Labeling Rule goes into effect
	Free Annual Credit Report Rule goes into effect
	First spyware case: <u>FTC v. Seismic Entertainment</u>
	FTC charges company with exposing consumers' purchases: <u>In the Matter of MTS (dba Tower Records)</u>
	FTC charges company with renting consumer information it had pledged to keep private: <u>In the Matter of Gateway Learning</u>

FTC issues *The CAN-SPAM Act of 2003: National Do Not Email Registry: A Federal Trade Commission Report to Congress*

FTC sponsors workshops: *Monitoring Software on Your PC: Spyware, Adware and Other Software; Radio Frequency IDentification: Applications and Implications for Consumers;* and *Peer-to-Peer File-Sharing Technology: Consumer Protection and Competition Issues*

FTC publishes *The CAN-SPAM Act: A Compliance Guide for Business*

2005

FACTA Disposal Rule goes into effect

FACTA Pre-Screen Opt Out Rule goes into effect

National Do Not Call Registry tops 100 million phone numbers

First Do Not Call enforcement action: FTC v. National Consumer Council

First Do Not Call civil penalty action: US v. Braglia Marketing

Highest civil penalty in a Do Not Call case: US v. DirecTV ($5.3 million)

First enforcement actions under Gramm-Leach-Bliley Safeguards Rule: In the Matter of Sunbelt Lending and In the Matter of Nationwide Mortgage Group

First unfairness allegation in a data security case: In the Matter of BJ's Wholesale Club

FTC issues *RFID: Radio Frequency IDentification: Applications and Implications for Consumers: A Workshop Report From the Staff of the Federal Trade Commission*

FTC issues *Spyware Workshop: Monitoring Software On Your Personal Computer: Spyware, Adware, and Other Software: Report of the Federal Trade Commission Staff*

FTC launches online safety website: OnGuardOnline.gov

2006

FACTA Rule Limiting Marketing Solicitations from Affiliates goes into effect

Highest civil penalty in a consumer protection case: US v. ChoicePoint ($10 million civil penalty for violations of FCRA as well as $5 million redress for victims)

First adware case: In the Matter of Zango

Highest civil penalty to date in a COPPA case: US v. Xanga ($1 million)

FTC settles charges against a payment processor that had experienced the largest breach of financial data to date: In the Matter of CardSystems Solutions

FTC issues *Peer-to-Peer File-Sharing Technology: Consumer Protection and Competition Issues: A Federal Trade Commission Staff Workshop Report*

FTC sponsors workshop: *Protecting Consumers in the Next Tech-Ade*

FTC launches national educational campaign on identity theft and publishes *Deter, Detect, Defend: Avoid ID Theft* brochure

FTC Privacy Milestones

continued

2007	First Disposal Rule case: <u>US v. American United Mortgage Company</u>
	Adult-oriented online social networking operation settles FTC charges; unwitting consumers pelted with sexually graphic pop-ups: <u>FTC v. Various (dba AdultFriendFinder)</u>
	FTC issues *Spam Summit: The Next Generation of Threats and Solutions: A Staff Report by the Federal Trade Commission's Division of Marketing Practices*
	FTC issues *Implementing the Children's Online Privacy Protection Act: A Federal Trade Commission Report to Congress*
	FTC co-chairs President's Identity Theft Task Force (with DOJ) and issues Strategic Plan
	FTC sponsors workshops: *Security in Numbers: SSNs and ID Theft; Ehavioral Advertising: Tracking, Targeting, and Technology*; and *Spam Summit: The Next Generation of Threats and Solutions*
	FTC publishes *Protecting Personal Information: A Guide for Business* and launches interactive tutorial
2008	Highest civil penalty in a CAN-SPAM case: <u>US v. ValueClick</u> ($2.9 million)
	FTC settles charges against data broker Lexis Nexis and retailer TJX related to the compromise of hundreds of thousands of consumers' information: <u>In the Matter of Reed Elsevier and Seisent</u> and <u>In the Matter of TJX Companies</u>
	FTC issues *Protecting Consumers in the Next Tech-ade: A Report by the Staff of the Federal Trade Commission*
	FTC issues *Security In Numbers: Social Security Numbers and Identity Theft – A Federal Trade Commission Report Providing Recommendations On Social Security Number Use In the Private Sector*
	President's Identity Theft Task Force Report released
	FTC sponsors workshops: *Protecting Personal Information: Best Practices for Business* (Chicago, Dallas, and Los Angeles); *Pay on the Go: Consumers and Contactless Payment, Transatlantic RFID Workshop on Consumer Privacy and Data Security*; and *Beyond Voice: Mapping the Mobile Marketplace*
	U.S. Postal Service sends FTC ID Theft prevention brochure to every household in the country
2009	Robocall Rule goes into effect
	Health Breach Notification Rule goes into effect
	First case alleging failure to protect employee information: <u>In the Matter of CVS Caremark</u>
	First cases alleging six companies violated the EU-US Safe Harbor Agreement: <u>In the Matter of World Innovators</u>, <u>In the Matter of ExpatEdge Partners</u>, <u>In the Matter of Onyx Graphics</u>, <u>In the Matter of Directors Desk</u>, <u>In the Matter of Progressive Gaitways</u>, and <u>In the Matter of Collectify</u>
	FTC issues *Self-Regulatory Principles For Online Behavioral Advertising: Tracking, Targeting, and Technology*

FTC sponsors workshops: *Exploring Privacy: A Roundtable Series*; *Protecting Personal Information: Best Practices for Business* (New York); and *Securing Personal Data in the Global Economy*

FTC publishes *Net Cetera: Chatting with Kids About Being Online*

2010

FTC jointly publishes Model Privacy Form under the Gramm-Leach-Bliley Act

National Do Not Call Registry tops 200 million phone numbers

First data security case involving social media: In the Matter of Twitter

First case shutting down a rogue ISP: FTC v. Pricewert

First data security case against an online seal provider: FTC v. ControlScan

Highest judgment in a spyware case: FTC v. Innovative Marketing ($163 million)

Largest FTC-state coordinated settlement on privacy: FTC v. Lifelock

FTC conducts sweep against companies for exposure of employee and/or customer data on peer-to-peer (P2P) file-sharing networks

FTC releases Preliminary FTC Staff Report *Protecting Consumer Privacy in an Era of Rapid Change: A Proposed Framework for Businesses and Policymakers*

FTC sponsors *COPPA Rule Review Roundtable*

FTC publishes *Peer-to-Peer File Sharing: A Guide for Businesses*; *Medical Identity Theft: How to Minimize Your Risk*; and *Copier Data Security: A Guide for Businesses*

FTC distributes 6+ million printed copies of *Deter, Detect, Defend: Avoid ID Theft* brochures and 5+ million printed copies of *Net Cetera: Chatting with Kids About Being Online*

2011

FTC seeks comment on proposed changes to COPPA rule

First case alleging substantive Safe Harbor violation and imposing privacy assessment program and audit requirements: In the Matter of Google

First case against an online advertising network for offering deceptive privacy controls: In the Matter of Chitika

First COPPA case against a mobile application developer: US v. W3 Innovations

First case alleging unfairness based on default privacy settings: FTC v. Frostwire

Largest FTC privacy case to date: In the Matter of Facebook

FTC releases report *40 Years of Experience with the Fair Credit Reporting Act*

FTC co-hosts *Stolen Futures: A Forum on Child ID Theft*

FTC hosts *Face Facts: A Forum on Facial Recognition* Workshop

FTC publishes *Tips for Using Public Wireless Networks*

FTC publishes *Facts from the FTC: What You Should Know About Mobile Apps*

FTC publishes *Online Safety for Teens and Tweens*

FTC Privacy Milestones

Laws & Rules ● Workshops
● Cases ● Education
● Reports

2012	FTC releases report *Using FACTA Remedies: An FTC Staff Report on a Survey of Identity Theft Victims*
	FTC releases report *Mobile Apps for Kids: Current Privacy Disclosures Are Disappointing*
	FTC announces workshop: *Paper, Plastic... or Mobile? An FTC Workshop on Mobile Payments*
	FTC announces workshop to Explore Disclosures in Online and Mobile Media
	FTC publishes Blog Post: *FCRA & Mobile Apps: A Word of Warning*

Personal Data Ecosystem

Personal Data Ecosystem

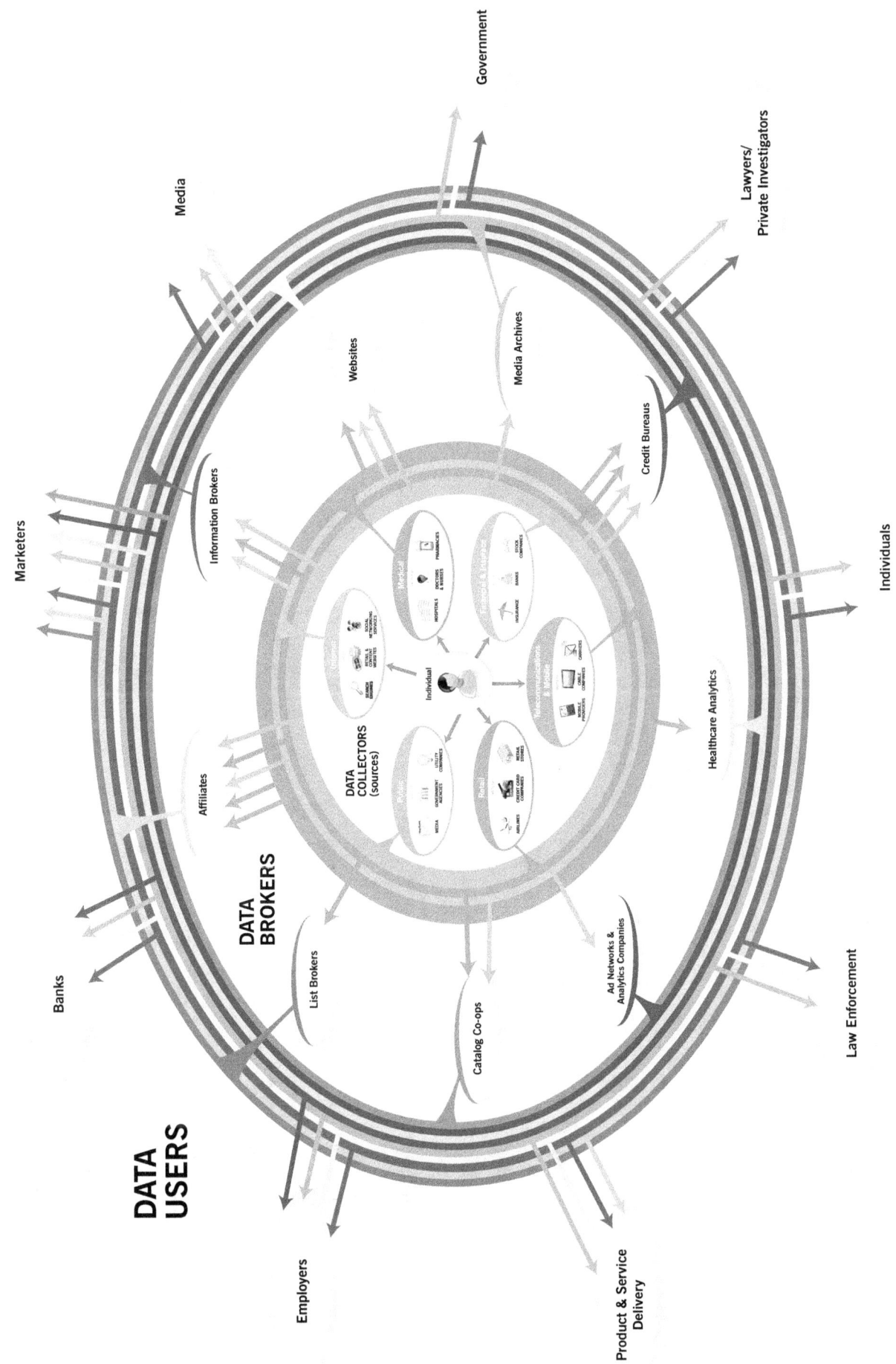

DATA
USERS

DATA
BROKERS

DATA
COLLECTORS
(sources)

Individual

Government

Media

Websites

Media Archives

Credit Bureaus

Information Brokers

Marketers

Individuals

Affiliates

Banks

Healthcare Analytics

List Brokers

Catalog Co-ops

Ad Networks &
Analytics Companies

Law Enforcement

Employers

Product & Service
Delivery

Lawyers/
Private Investigators

DATA USES:

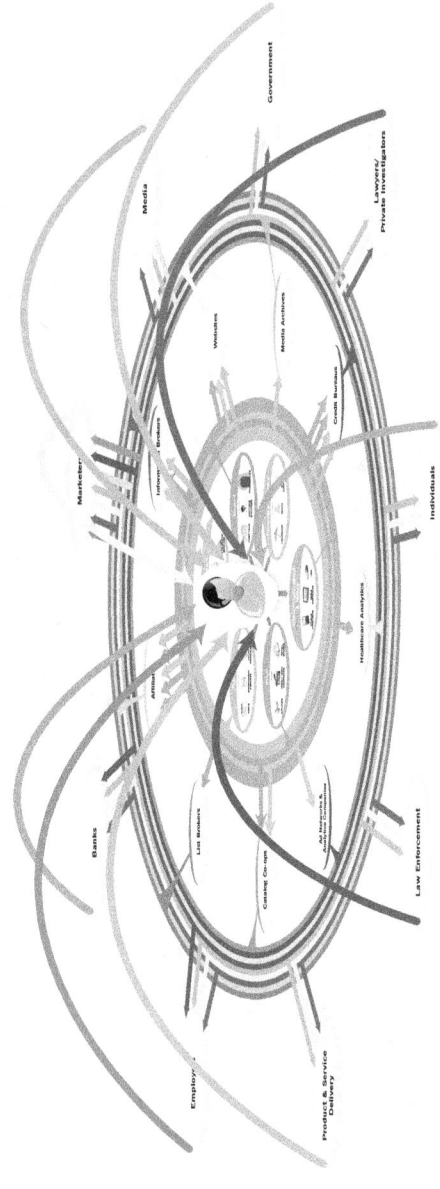

Examples of uses of consumer information in personally identifiable or aggregated form:

- Financial services, such as for banking or investment accounts

- Credit granting, such as for credit or debit cards; mortgage, automobile or specialty loans; automobile rentals; or telephone services

- Insurance granting, such as for health, automobile or life

- Retail coupons and special offers

- Catalog and magazine solicitations

- Web and mobile services, including content, e-mail, search, and social networking

- Product and service delivery, such as streaming video, package delivery, or a cable signal

- Attorneys, such as for case investigations

- Journalism, such as for fact checking

- Marketing, whether electronically, through direct mail, or by telephone

- Data brokers for aggregation and resale to companies and/or consumers

- Background investigations by employers or landlords

- Locating missing or lost persons, beneficiaries, or witnesses

- Law enforcement

- Research (e.g., health, financial, and online search data) by academic institutions, government agencies, and commercial companies

- Fraud detection and prevention

- Government benefits and services, such as licensing

Dissenting Statement of Commissioner J. Thomas Rosch

Introduction

I agree in several respects with what the "final" Privacy Report says. Specifically, although I disagree that the consumer has traditionally ever been given any "choice" about information collection practices (other than to "take-it-or-leave-it" after reviewing a firm's privacy notice), I agree that consumers ought to be given a broader range of choices if for no other reason than to customize their privacy protection. However, I still worry about the constitutionality of banning take-it-or-leave-it choice (in circumstances where the consumer has few alternatives); as a practical matter, that prohibition may chill information collection, and thus impact innovation, regardless whether one's privacy policy is deceptive or not.[1]

I also applaud the Report's recommendation that Congress enact "targeted" legislation giving consumers "access" to correct misinformation about them held by a data broker.[2] I also support the Report's recommendation that Congress implement federal legislation that would require entities to maintain reasonable security and to notify consumers in the event of certain security breaches.[3]

Finally, I concur with the Report insofar as it recommends that information brokers who compile data for marketing purposes must disclose to consumers how they collect and use consumer data.[4] I have long felt that we had no business counseling Congress or other agencies about privacy concerns without that information. Although I have suggested that compulsory process be used to obtain such information (because I am convinced that is the only way to ensure that our information is complete and accurate),[5] a voluntary centralized website is arguably a step in the right direction.

Privacy Framework

My disagreement with the "final" Privacy Report is fourfold. First, the Report is rooted in its insistence that the "unfair" prong, rather than the "deceptive" prong, of the Commission's Section 5 consumer protection statute, should govern information gathering practices (including "tracking"). "Unfairness" is an elastic and elusive concept. What is "unfair" is in the eye of the beholder. For example, most consumer advocacy groups consider behavioral tracking to be unfair, whether or not the information being tracked is personally identifiable ("PII") and regardless of the circumstances under which an entity does the

---

1   *Protecting Consumer Privacy in an Era of Rapid Change: Recommendations for Businesses and Policymakers* ("Report") at 50-52.

2   *Id.* at 14, 73.

3   *Id.* at 26. I also support the recommendation that such legislation authorize the Commission to seek civil penalties for violations. However, despite its bow to "targeted" legislation, the Report elsewhere counsels that the Commission support privacy legislation generally. *See, e.g., id.* at 16. To the extent that those recommendations are not defined, or narrowly targeted, I disagree with them.

4   *Id.* at 14, 68-70.

5   *See* J. Thomas Rosch, Comm'r, Fed. Trade Comm'n, Information and Privacy: In Search of a Data-Driven Policy, Remarks at the Technology Policy Institute Aspen Forum (Aug. 22, 2011), *available at* http://www.ftc.gov/speeches/rosch/110822aspeninfospeech.pdf.

tracking. But, as I have said, consumer surveys are inconclusive, and individual consumers by and large do not "opt out" from tracking when given the chance to do so.[6] Not surprisingly, large enterprises in highly concentrated industries, which may be tempted to raise the privacy bar so high that it will disadvantage rivals, also support adopting more stringent privacy principles.[7]

The "final" Privacy Report (incorporating the preliminary staff report) repeatedly sides with consumer organizations and large enterprises. It proceeds on the premise that behavioral tracking is "unfair."[8] Thus, the Report expressly recommends that "reputational harm" be considered a type of harm that the Commission should redress.[9] The Report also expressly says that privacy be the default setting for commercial data practices.[10] Indeed, the Report says that the "traditional distinction between PII and non-PII has blurred,"[11] and it recommends "shifting the burdens away from consumers and placing obligations on businesses."[12] To the extent the Report seeks consistency with international privacy standards,[13] I would urge caution. We should always carefully consider whether each individual policy choice regarding privacy is appropriate for this country in all contexts.

That is not how the Commission itself has traditionally proceeded. To the contrary, the Commission represented in its 1980, and 1982, Statements to Congress that, absent deception, it will not generally enforce Section 5 against alleged intangible harm.[14] In other contexts, the Commission has tried, through its advocacy, to convince others that our policy judgments are sensible and ought to be adopted. And, as I stated in connection with the recent *Intel* complaint, in the competition context, one of the principal virtues

---

6   *See* Katy Bachman, *Study: Internet User Adoption of DNT Hard to Predict*, adweek.com, March 20, 2012, *available at* http://www.adweek.com/news/technology/study-internet-user-adoption-dnt-hard-predict-139091 (reporting on a survey that found that what Internet users say they are going to do about using a Do Not Track button and what they are currently doing about blocking tracking on the Internet, are two different things); *see also* Concurring Statement of Commissioner J. Thomas Rosch, Issuance of Preliminary FTC Staff Report "Protecting Consumer Privacy in an Era of Rapid Change: A Proposed Framework for Businesses and Policymakers" (Dec. 1, 2010), *available at* http://www.ftc.gov/speeches/rosch/101201privacyreport.pdf.

7   *See* J. Thomas Rosch, Comm'r, Fed. Trade Comm'n, Do Not Track: Privacy in an Internet Age, Remarks at Loyola Chicago Antitrust Institute Forum, (Oct. 14, 2011), *available at* http://www.ftc.gov/speeches/rosch/111014-dnt-loyola.pdf; *see also* Report at 9.

8   Report at 8 and n.37.

9   *Id.* at 2. The Report seems to imply that the Do Not Call Rule would support this extension of the definition of harm. *See id.* ("unwarranted intrusions into their daily lives"). However, it must be emphasized that the *Congress* granted the FTC underlying authority under the Telemarketing and Consumer Fraud and Abuse Prevention Act, 15 U.S.C. §§ 6101-6108, to promulgate the Do Not Call provisions and other substantial amendments to the TSR. The Commission did not do so unilaterally.

10   *Id.*

11   *Id.* at 19.

12   *Id.* at 23, *see also id.* at 24.

13   *Id.* at 9-10. This does not mean that I am an isolationist or am impervious to the benefits of a global solution. But, as stated below, there is more than one way to skin this cat.

14   *See* Letter from the FTC to Hon. Wendell Ford and Hon. John Danforth, Committee on Commerce, Science and Transportation, United States Senate, Commission Statement of Policy on the Scope of Consumer Unfairness Jurisdiction (Dec. 17, 1980), reprinted in International Harvester Co., 104 F.T.C. 949, 1070, 1073 (1984) ("Unfairness Policy Statement") *available at* http://www.ftc.gov/bcp/policystmt/ad-unfair.htm; Letter from the FTC to Hon. Bob Packwood and Hon. Bob Kasten, Committee on Commerce, Science and Transportation, United States Senate, reprinted in FTC Antitrust & Trade Reg. Rep. (BNA) 1055, at 568-570 ("Packwood-Kasten letter"); and 15 U.S.C. § 45(n), which codified the FTC's modern approach.

of applying Section 5 was that that provision was "self-limiting," and I advocated that Section 5 be applied on a stand-alone basis only to a firm with monopoly or near-monopoly power.[15] Indeed, as I have remarked, absent such a limiting principle, privacy may be used as a weapon by firms having monopoly or near-monopoly power.[16]

There does not appear to be any such limiting principle applicable to many of the recommendations of the Report. If implemented as written, many of the Report's recommendations would instead apply to almost all firms and to most information collection practices. It would install "Big Brother" as the watchdog over these practices not only in the online world but in the offline world.[17] That is not only paternalistic, but it goes well beyond what the Commission said in the early 1980s that it would do, and well beyond what Congress has permitted the Commission to do under Section 5(n).[18] I would instead stand by what we have said and challenge information collection practices, including behavioral tracking, only when these practices are deceptive, "unfair" within the strictures of Section 5(n) and our commitments to Congress, or employed by a firm with market power and therefore challengeable on a stand-alone basis under Section 5's prohibition of unfair methods of competition.

Second, the current self-regulation and browser mechanisms for implementing Do Not Track solutions may have advanced since the issuance of the preliminary staff Report.[19] But, as the final Report concedes, they are far from perfect,[20] and they may never be, despite efforts to create a standard through the World Wide Web Consortium ("W3C") for the browser mechanism.[21]

More specifically, as I have said before, the major browser firms' interest in developing Do Not Track mechanisms begs the question of whether and to what extent those major browser firms will act strategically and opportunistically (to use privacy to protect their own entrenched interests).[22]

In addition, the recent announcement by the Digital Advertising Alliance (DAA) that it will honor the tracking choices consumers make through their browsers raises more questions than answers for me. The Report is not clear, and I am concerned, about the extent to which this latest initiative will displace the standard-setting effort that has recently been undertaken by the W3C. Furthermore, it is not clear that all the interested players in the Do Not Track arena – whether it be the DAA, the browser firms, the W3C, or consumer advocacy groups – will be able to come to agreement about what "Do Not Track" even means.[23] It may be that the firms professing an interest in self-regulation are really talking about a "Do Not Target" mechanism, which would only prevent a firm from serving targeted ads, rather than a "Do Not Track"

---

15 *See* Concurring and Dissenting Statement of Commissioner J. Thomas Rosch, *In re Intel Corp.*, Docket No. 9341, (Dec. 16, 2009), *available at* http://www.ftc.gov/os/adjpro/d9341/091216intelstatement.pdf.

16 *See* Rosch, *supra* note 7 at 20.

17 *See* Report at 13.

18 Federal Trade Commission Act Amendments of 1994, Pub. L. No. 103-312.

19 Report at 4, 52.

20 *Id.* at 53, 54; *see esp. id.* at 53 n.250.

21 *Id.* at 5, 54.

22 *See* Rosch, *supra* note 7 at 20-21.

23 Tony Romm, "*What Exactly Does 'Do Not Track' Mean?*," Politico, Mar. 13, 2012, *available at* http://www.politico.com/news/stories/0312/73976.html; *see also* Report at 4 (DAA allows consumer to opt out of "targeted advertising").

mechanism, which would prevent the collection of consumer data altogether. For example, the DAA's Self-Regulatory Principles for Multi-Site Data do not apply to data collected for "market research" or "product development."[24] For their part, the major consumer advocacy groups may not be interested in a true "Do Not Track" mechanism either. They may only be interested in a mechanism that prevents data brokers from compiling consumer profiles instead of a comprehensive solution. It is hard to see how the W3C can adopt a standard unless and until there is an agreement about what the standard is supposed to prevent.[25]

It is also not clear whether or to what extent the lessons of the Carnegie Mellon Study respecting the lack of consumer understanding of how to access and use Do Not Track will be heeded.[26] Similarly, it is not clear whether and to what extent Commissioner Brill's concern that consumers' choices, whether it be "Do Not Collect" or merely "Do Not Target," will be honored.[27] Along the same lines, it is also not clear whether and to what extent a "partial" Do Not Track solution (offering nuanced choice) will be offered or whether it is "all or nothing." Indeed, it is not clear whether consumers can or will be given complete and accurate information about the pros and the cons of subscribing to Do Not Track before they choose it. I find this last question especially vexing in light of a recent study that indicated 84% of users polled prefer targeted advertising in exchange for free online content.[28]

Third, I am concerned that "opt-in" will necessarily be selected as the *de facto* method of consumer choice for a wide swath of entities that have a first-party relationship with consumers but who can potentially track consumers' activities across unrelated websites, under circumstances where it is unlikely, because of the "context" (which is undefined) for such tracking to be "consistent" (which is undefined) with that first-party relationship:[29] 1) companies with multiple lines of business that allow data collection in different contexts (such as Google);[30] 2) "social networks," (such as Facebook and Twitter), which could potentially use "cookies," "plug-ins," applications, or other mechanisms to track a consumer's activities across

---

24 See *Self-Regulatory Principles for Multi-Site Data*, Digital Advertising Alliance, Nov. 2011, at 3, 10, 11, *available at* http://www.aboutads.info/resource/download/Multi-Site-Data-Principles.pdf; *see also* Tanzina Vega, *Opt-Out Provision Would Halt Some, but Not All, Web Tracking*, New York Times, Feb. 26, 2012, *available at* http://www.nytimes.com/2012/02/27/technology/opt-out-provision-would-halt-some-but-not-all-web-tracking.html?pagewanted=all.

25 See Vega, *supra* note 24.

26 *"Why Johnny Can't Opt Out: A Usability Evaluation of Tools to Limit Online Behavioral Advertising,"* Carnegie Mellon University CyLab, Oct. 31, 2011, *available at* http://www.cylab.cmu.edu/files/pdfs/tech_reports/CMUCyLab11017.pdf; *see also Search Engine Use 2012*, at 25, Pew Internet & American Life Project, Pew Research Center, Mar. 9, 2012, *available at* http://pewinternet.org/~/media/Files/Reports/2012/PIP_Search_Engine_Use_2012.pdf ("[j]ust 38% of internet users say they are generally aware of ways they themselves can limit how much information about them is collected by a website").

27 See Julie Brill, Comm'r, Fed. Trade Comm'n, Big Data, Big Issues, Remarks at Fordham University School of Law (Mar. 2, 2012) *available at* http://www.ftc.gov/speeches/brill/120228fordhamlawschool.pdf.

28 See Bachman, *supra* note 6.

29 Report at 41.

30 *Id.* Notwithstanding that Google's prospective conduct seems to fit perfectly the circumstances set forth on this page of the Report (describing a company with multiple lines of business including a search engine and ad network), where the Commission states "consumer choice" is warranted, the Report goes on to conclude on page 56 that Google's practices do not require affirmative express consent because they "currently are not so widespread that they could track a consumer's every movement across the Internet."

the Internet;[31] and 3) "retargeters," (such as Amazon or Pacers), which include a retailer who delivers an ad on a third-party website based on the consumer's previous activity on the retailer's website.[32]

These entities might have to give consumers "opt-in" choice now or in the future: 1) regardless whether the entity's privacy policy and notices adequately describe the information collection practices at issue; 2) regardless of the sensitivity of the information being collected; 3) regardless whether the consumer cares whether "tracking" is actually occurring; 4) regardless of the entity's market position (whether the entity can use privacy strategically – *i.e.*, an opt-in requirement – in order to cripple or eliminate a rival); and 5) conversely, regardless whether the entity can compete effectively or innovate, as a practical matter, if it must offer "opt in" choice.[33]

Fourth, I question the Report's apparent mandate that ISPs, with respect to uses of deep packet inspection, be required to use opt-in choice.[34] This is not to say there is no basis for requiring ISPs to use opt-in choice without requiring opt-in choice for other large platform providers. But that kind of "discrimination" cannot be justified, as the Report says, because ISPs have "are in a position to develop highly detailed and comprehensive profiles of their customers."[35] So does any large platform provider who makes available a browser or operating system to consumers.[36]

Nor can that "discrimination" be justified on the ground that ISPs may potentially use that data to "track" customer behavior in a fashion that is contrary to consumer expectations. There is no reliable data establishing that most ISPs presently do so. Indeed, with a business model based on subscription revenue, ISPs arguably lack the same incentives as do other platform providers whose business model is based on attracting advertising and advertising revenue: ISPs assert that they track data only to perform operational and security functions; whereas other platform providers that have business models based on advertising revenue track data in order to maximize their advertising revenue.

What really distinguishes ISPs from most other "large platform providers" is that their markets can be highly concentrated.[37] Moreover, even when an ISP operates in a less concentrated market, switching costs can be, or can be perceived as being, high.[38] As I said in connection with the *Intel* complaint, a monopolist or near monopolist may have obligations which others do not have.[39] The only similarly situated platform provider may be Google, which, because of its alleged monopoly power in the search advertising market,

---

31 *Id.* at 40. *See also supra* note 30. That observation also applies to "social networks" like Facebook.

32 *Id.* at 41.

33 *See id.* at 60 ("Final Principle").

34 *Id.* at 56 ("the Commission has strong concerns about the use of DPI for purposes inconsistent with an ISP's interaction with a consumer, without express affirmative consent or more robust protection").

35 *Id.*

36 *Id.*

37 Federal Communications Commission, *Connecting America: The National Broadband Plan, Broadband Competition and Innovation Policy, Section 4.1, Networks, Competition in Residential Broadband Markets* at 36, *available at* http://www. broadband.gov/plan/4-broadband-competition-and-innovation-policy/.

38 Federal Communications Commission Working Paper, *Broadband decisions: What drives consumers to switch – or stick with – their broadband Internet provider* (Dec. 2010), at 3, 8, *available at* http://transition.fcc.gov/Daily_Releases/Daily_ Business/2010/db1206/DOC-303264A1.pdf.

39 *See* Rosch, *supra* note 15.

has similar power. For any of these "large platform providers," however, affirmative express consent should be required only when the provider *actually* wants to use the data in this fashion, not just when it *has the potential* to do so.[40]

Conclusion

Although the Chairman testified recently before the House Appropriations Subcommittee chaired by Congresswoman Emerson that the recommendations of the final Report are supposed to be nothing more than "best practices,"[41] I am concerned that the language of the Report indicates otherwise, and broadly hints at the prospect of enforcement.[42] The Report also acknowledges that it is intended to serve as a template for legislative recommendations.[43] Moreover, to the extent that the Report's "best practices" mirror the Administration's privacy "Bill of Rights," the President has specifically asked either that the "Bill of Rights" be adopted by the Congress or that they be distilled into "enforceable codes of conduct."[44] As I testified before the same subcommittee, this is a "tautology;" either these practices are to be adopted voluntarily by the firms involved or else there is a federal requirement that they be adopted, in which case there can be no pretense that they are "voluntary."[45] It makes no difference whether the federal requirement is in the form of enforceable codes of conduct or in the form of an act of Congress. Indeed, it is arguable that neither is needed if these firms feel obliged to comply with the "best practices" or face the wrath of "the Commission" or its staff.

---

40 *See, e.g.*, Report at 56.

41 Testimony of Jon Leibowitz and J. Thomas Rosch, Chairman and Comm'r, FTC, *The FTC in FY2013: Protecting Consumers and Competition: Hearing on Budget Before the H. Comm. on Appropriations Subcomm. on Financial Services and General Government*, 112th Cong. 2 (2012), text from CQ Roll Call, available from: LexisNexis® Congressional.

42 One notable example is found where the Report discusses the articulation of privacy harms and enforcement actions brought on the basis of *deception*. The Report then notes "[l]ike these enforcement actions, a privacy framework should address practices that unexpectedly reveal previously private information even absent physical or financial harm, or unwarranted intrusions." Report at 8. The accompanying footnote concludes that "even in the absence of such misrepresentations, revealing previously-private consumer data could cause consumer harm." *See also infra* note 43.

43 *Id.* at 16 ("to the extent Congress enacts any of the Commission's recommendations through legislation"); *see also id.* at 12-13 ("the Commission calls on Congress to develop baseline privacy legislation that is technologically neutral and sufficiently flexible to allow companies to continue to innovate").

44 *See* Letter from President Barack Obama, *appended to* White House, *Consumer Data Privacy in a Networked World: A Framework for Protecting Privacy and Promoting Innovation in the Global Digital Economy* (Feb. 23, 2012), *available at* http://www.whitehouse.gov/sites/default/files/privacy-final.pdf.

45 *See* FTC Testimony, *supra* note 41.

www.ingramcontent.com/pod-product-compliance
Lightning Source LLC
Chambersburg PA
CBHW080821180526
45168CB00006B/2537